2-6-22

Doug & Terri,
Blessings to you,
& welcome home!
James +

BOLD TO SAY

Reflections on the Lord's Prayer

Library of Congress Cataloging-in-Publication Data

Names: Jones, Rachel (Editor), editor.
Title: Bold to say : reflections on the Lord's prayer / edited by Rachel Jones ; with Cohen Adkins, Ryan Black, James Derkits, Elizabeth DeRuff, Miriam McKenney, Catherine Meeks, Sandra Montes, and Sam Portara.
Description: Cincinnati, Ohio : Forward Movement, 2021. | Summary: "When Jesus teaches his disciples to pray, he keeps it simple, offering fewer than 100 words to form the Lord's Prayer. Despite its brevity, the Lord's Prayer presents a profound framework for our relationship to God and a model for how we ought to pray and live. From the first word to the last, the prayer calls us to reorient ourselves and our lives back into God's goodness and will. This collection of essays explores each line of the Lord's Prayer and provides insight into how we, like the disciples, may be bold to say and live into these words of petition and praise"-- Provided by publisher.
Identifiers: LCCN 2021019941 (print) | LCCN 2021019942 (ebook) | ISBN 9780880284875 (paperback) | ISBN 9780880284875 (ebook)
Subjects: LCSH: Lord's prayer--Meditations.
Classification: LCC BV230 .B6346 2021 (print) | LCC BV230 (ebook) | DDC 226.9/6--dc23
LC record available at https://lccn.loc.gov/2021019941
LC ebook record available at https://lccn.loc.gov/2021019942

Cover: "I Wonder If I Pray," a painting by Shelley Bain. To see more of her artwork, visit shelleybain.com.

ISBN: 978-0-88028-487-5

BOLD TO SAY

Reflections on the Lord's Prayer

Edited by Rachel Jones

With Cohen Adkins, Ryan Black, James Derkits,
Elizabeth DeRuff, Miriam McKenney, Catherine Meeks,
Sandra Montes, and Sam Portaro

Forward Movement
Cincinnati, Ohio

TABLE OF CONTENTS

INTRODUCTION

INTRODUCTION

Over and over again in the pages of the Bible, God shows us what love looks like in the good brown soil, the bright blue sky, the big yellow sun, and all that grows and creeps upon the earth. None of that is accidental. We are made of the dust of the earth and God's goodness keeps drawing us back to each other—back to the very basics of ourselves and our faith.

When Jesus teaches his disciples to pray, he keeps it simple. Jesus's model for how we ought to pray is a study in the struggle to keep God at the center of our busy minds and lives. If there ever was a centering prayer, the Lord's Prayer is surely one. From the first word to the last, we are reorienting ourselves and our lives back into God's goodness and will. It is a painfully honest, deeply human prayer.

I can't tell you when I learned the Lord's Prayer, but I know my mother and father regularly prayed it with me. All I can tell you is that I can remember praying it for as long as I have known what praying was, prayed it in church as long as I have known what church was, prayed along with it at every pivotal moment of my life. I expect to meet Jesus with this prayer on my lips.

One of my previous church-lady lives included sharing communion with very old or very sick (and sometimes both) people. I also spent a great deal of time doing chapel with very small, very young children. Those two stages of life are not nearly as far apart as any of us imagine. The Lord's Prayer was a central focus of much of my liturgical life with both of these communities.

Cleo's hands were practically see-through by the time I knew her. She was a feisty firecracker of a lady with sparkly blue eyes who loved to tell me about the time she danced with Lawrence Welk. "The bubble machine smelled just awful, but that man…he could dance." She would puff it out in little chuffs and whistles, so tickled and trying so hard to conserve her breath. By the time she turned 85, Cleo's lungs were mostly rusted steel wool and chalk dust, so if she could muster up the wind to tell you something at full volume, you paid attention. And Cleo loved to say the Lord's Prayer at full volume. It cost her so much to do it. She would pant these short little puffs, and I would wait until she caught her breath to offer her the bread and wine. She never missed the chance to pray, even when all she could do was move her lips along with the words. And she would hold my hand and squeeze it when we got to Amen.

Jackson's hands could not have been more different from Cleo's. They were usually full (or recently emptied) of something sticky and slightly warm. His lifelines were colored in by playground dirt, and his upper lip was stained with grape juice. Jackson looked like one of the round, angelic putti had flown down from the walls of the Vatican and landed smack in the middle of my morning children's chapel. He was angelic in appearance and built like a very small Mack truck. Jackson and Cleo probably weighed about the same and enjoyed all the same snacks. And like Cleo, Jackson loved to pray at full volume, if not louder. He was ardent in his prayer, eyes squeezed tightly, little biscuit hands clasped to his chest. I heard him ask God to "weed us not into ten stations, but delibber us from eagles..." and I had to choke back one of those laughing sobs that are gifts of the Holy Spirit.

Cleo was well aware of the weight of the words she was praying, and precious Jackson had only just begun to understand what words were at all. But the prayer Jesus gave us was one they both knew and loved.

I have prayed the Lord's Prayer my whole life, individually and in groups, sometimes paying rapt attention to every word and syllable, other times just stumbling and mumbling along, and sometimes just being still with the words in my head or coming from the voices around me. I knew it was a good prayer, maybe even the best prayer, but having received my early Christian formation in a tradition that placed a high value on spontaneous prayer, part of me worried that I was kind of cheating if that's all I did.

And then one night in 2007, in a church yard where I was a stranger leaning deeply into the hospitality of strangers and with a belly full of spicy hominy and pork stew called *pozole,* when the fatigue and joy of hard work and summer heat and Jesus's broken body and my broken Spanish all coalesced into my own private kind of Pentecost. I mostly knew where we were in the eucharist service, and as we transitioned into the Liturgy of the Table, I started to cry. By the time we got to the Lord's Prayer, I was stifling sobs. It was a moment of holy mystery and communion unlike any other I've had.

To be set right, to insist and ask that God's will be made manifest in our lives in a community that is bound together beyond language or custom, is a powerful event. It shook my world, and nothing has ever been the same.

When we began pulling the threads of this book together, the world looked very different. 2019 doesn't seem like so long ago, but sometimes the world moves on quickly, and we spend a significant amount of time catching our breath. In the weeks and months of quarantine that followed the outbreak of COVID-19, our lives radically changed. Efforts to keep each other safe and to protect especially vulnerable people in our communities required extreme measures. We had to learn how to do something none of us have much practice doing—being alone together.

Because God is always in the business of teaching us how to love each other and how to be love in the world, this prayer from Jesus's heart has been a way for us to be together in our separation from loved ones, work and school friends, and our worship communities. I can imagine that, as the disciples carried the Lord's Prayer in their hearts through the rest of their lives, preaching the Good News of God in Christ, they realized over and over again how much this prayer set them up to live simple, truthful, honest, and loving lives.

One of the most beautiful things about the Lord's Prayer is that it constantly reminds us of our place in community, of our connectedness, and of our dependence on each other. We place ourselves into the keeping of God's will rather than our own. We ask for enough to keep our bodies alive for just one more day, and we forgive one another. We recognize that all of us are tempted and that God's goodness and mercy is the only thing that can save us from all the trials we face, and we remind ourselves that God's sovereignty and glory and timelessness hold all of us together in a love that is deeper and wider than we could ask or imagine.

In the Episcopal liturgy of Holy Eucharist, we lead-in to the prayer with the words, "We are bold to say." This simple but profound phrase reminds us that this is a bold prayer, and we would do well to remember that. The Lord's Prayer is not just a nice set of words stitched on samplers or painted on chancels or memorialized in Tiffany glass windows. It's a deadly serious prayer and praying it with real intent will change your life. I know it has changed mine—and will continue to change me.

Indeed, working on this project about the Lord's Prayer changed my life—and not just because it required me to be mindful of this prayer in a different way than I'd been before. Writing about the Lord's Prayer and inviting others to do so is different than praying it with sweet old ladies or rowdy small boys, different than praying it during my own prayers or during staff meetings. What I have learned between the day the idea for this project emerged until the day it was complete could fill another book entirely. I thought I was planning a book about the Lord's Prayer, and that was gift enough. I had no idea that exploring this prayer would reveal wonders I didn't know to look out for, miracles of grace beyond my wildest dreams and farthest reckonings.

Like many of you, the Lord's Prayer is the prayer I pray when I don't know what to pray, when I can't sleep or concentrate, when things are coming hot and heavy and I need to center myself in God's goodness and boundless grace. Now that I'm fully middle-aged, I catch myself praying it at stoplights, when I have to turn around and go back to the house for something I forgot, in the shower when I start to rehash things that are better left in the delete bin, when it's all going in the right direction, and when it's all going straight to hell. Jesus says exactly what I ought to pray for, and his instructions to me have always been better than anything I could come up with on my own.

Every person who wrote for this book commented something to the effect of, "This was a lot harder than I thought it was going to be." Turns out that talking about this deeply beloved prayer is more difficult than we might imagine. It's not for lack of words or desire—it's just that once you start, it's hard to shut off. It's like being in love and not being able to stop talking about your beloved. Every time you talk about them, you get all cotton-mouthed and flushed, and then the words start rolling out, painting a word picture of what love looks like, and you hope on hope that you don't sound like an overly enthusiastic teenager with a major crush.

I am deeply grateful for each of the stories our authors have shared, for their willingness to be deeply vulnerable and real before God and all of us reading along, and for their love for Jesus and his people. Each of them has something precious to offer you, the Church, and the very heart of Jesus. I hope that you will remember them in your prayers as you journey beside them in this book. I asked each of these people to spend a significant amount of time with the prayer itself and included some passages from the Bible to augment and illustrate some of the bits we might otherwise not notice. I also sent along a playlist of songs for our writers to listen to as they read, prayed, and wrote. Each author was given the opportunity to tell you about how this prayer has changed the way they live their lives, the way they see the world, and how they follow Jesus. Some draw deeply on the passages at the beginning of the chapters, but they all preach a holy and whole gospel of their own.

Each phrase of the Lord's Prayer is represented with a separate chapter. We've included the same Bible passages we gave to our writers at the beginning of each chapter, with the exception of Judges 6-7, which seemed a bit excessive to reprint. Please do read that extra portion, though. It will add to the flavor of the chapter. We hope that you will write notes and comments all over this book and maybe even fill up a journal or two along the way. Much like the Lord's Prayer itself, we hope this book will become a trusted companion on your own journey of faith.

The famous Texas bluesman and itinerant preacher Blind Willie Johnson recorded a song called "Sweeter as the Years Go By," written by Ohio hatmaker and prodigious hymn writer Lelia Norris. It's an old song and has long been in the public domain. The lyrics are about Jesus, but as I've worked on this project and listened to this song, it has come to define how I feel about the Lord's Prayer, too. It's also become a prayer for the love I hope is kindled or rekindled in you, as you spend time in these pages with Jesus and the prayer he taught us.

Of Jesus's love that sought me, when I was lost in sin;
Of wondrous grace that brought me back to his fold again;
Of heights and depths of mercy, far deeper than the sea,
And higher than the heavens, my theme shall ever be.

Sweeter as the years go by,
Sweeter as the years go by,
Richer, fuller, deeper, Jesus's love is sweeter,
Sweeter as the years go by.

He trod in old Judea life's pathway long ago;
The people thronged about him, his saving grace to know;
He healed the brokenhearted, and caused the blind to see;
And still his great heart yearneth in love for even me.

Sweeter as the years go by,
Sweeter as the years go by,
Richer, fuller, deeper, Jesus's love is sweeter,
Sweeter as the years go by.

'Twas wondrous love which led him for us to suffer loss,
To bear without a murmur the anguish of the cross;
With saints redeemed in glory, let us our voices raise,
Till Heav'n and earth re-echo with our Redeemer's praise.

Sweeter as the years go by,
Sweeter as the years go by,
Richer, fuller, deeper, Jesus's love is sweeter,
Sweeter as the years go by.

With prayers for peace and joy,

Rachel Jones
Editor of *Bold to Say*

CHAPTER 1

Rend Your Hearts

The Word of the Lord

Yet even now, says the Lord*, return to me with all your heart, with fasting, with weeping, and with mourning; rend your hearts and not your clothing. Return to the* Lord*, your God, for he is gracious and merciful, slow to anger, and abounding in steadfast love, and relents from punishing. Who knows whether he will not turn and relent, and leave a blessing behind him, a grain offering and a drink offering for the* Lord*, your God?*

Blow the trumpet in Zion; sanctify a fast; call a solemn assembly; gather the people. Sanctify the congregation; assemble the aged; gather the children, even infants at the breast. Let the bridegroom leave his room, and the bride her canopy.

Between the vestibule and the altar let the priest, the minsters of the Lord*, weep. Let them say, "Spare you people, O* Lord*, and do not make your heritage a mockery, a byword among the nations. Why should it be said among the people, "Where is their God?"*

—Joel 2:12-17

While they were eating, [Jesus] took a loaf of bread, and after blessing it he broke it, gave it to them, and said, "Take; this is my body." Then he took a cup, and after giving thanks he gave it to them, and all of them drank from it. He said to them, "This is my blood of the covenant, which is poured out for many. Truly I tell you, I will never again drink of the fruit of the vine until that day when I drink it new in the kingdom of God."

—Mark 14:22-25

Our Father in heaven, hallowed be your Name

Miriam McKenney

Our Father in heaven

In 1995, Ann Arbor, Michigan, experienced one of the hottest summers in years. The temperatures rose to more than 100 degrees that July. It was the wrong time for the engine block to crack in my husband's Suzuki Sidekick, which meant he had to take my car to work in Livonia—thirty minutes away. My daughter, Nia, and I were home all day, alone together. She was perfect company, but at one-month-old, our conversations were mostly one-sided. Walking outdoors only broke out her entire precious little body in a heat rash.

The news on TV didn't help my postpartum depression. I felt trapped and alone all day, so I did what I always do when I don't know what to do. I called my dad.

"Hey, Dad, how's it going?" Our conversations always begin this way, and he always sounds glad to talk to me.

"HEY, keed, how're you doing?"

In our regular conversations, we'd talk and laugh, and he'd tell me what was going on at home with our family and at church. He always asked if I needed anything. If I had the courage to tell him, he'd help me with whatever it was. This time, I shared our car worries with him.

The next time we talked, he announced that he and my mom had decided to help us buy a new car. I began to cry. I hated asking him for help, and I hated needing help. But Dad didn't care. At the end of all of our conversations, he said the same thing, without fail. "Always remember—you have a dad."

Dad and I were close from the very beginning. My mom loved to show me photos of Dad and me together—even from the time I was a little baby—and tell me stories about all the places we would go. "He took you everywhere with him and you always wanted to go." Photos help to retain memories, and I have a few distinct memories of the two of us riding in his blue Volkswagen Beetle when I was three.

One day, we were driving through our little town of Wayne, Pennsylvania, when one of the car doors flew open. I remember a typewriter sitting on the back seat flying out of the car. Dad pulled over and ran to the side where I was sitting. I vividly remember him in his clericals, leaning into the car to check on me. What I remember most clearly was his panicked face atop his white collar and black clergy shirt. We were both scared, but I simultaneously felt completely safe. Years later, I asked him about this memory, and he told me that the typewriter didn't fall out of the car. Kid memories often contain revisionist history, but I had remembered the important part. My dad showed me then, as he shows me often, that he loves me.

Dad made it clear to us as kids that loving God came first. He felt his call to the priesthood as a teenager, and his faith was palpable. Dad's faith was one of practice more than discussion, so lots of what he did in practical terms was a mystery to me until I was much older. One of those mysteries was summed up in the prayer we had to memorize, one that I didn't understand—all I knew was that I had to be able to recite it by heart.

"Our Father, who art in heaven," my brothers and I would begin, confidently.

"Hallow… halloweh… hallowed be thy name?"

I had no idea what I was saying. But that didn't seem to matter. Learning the words felt right. I remember being so proud of myself when I could say it without reading it in the Book of Common Prayer at church. Memorizing that prayer led to my memorizing many other prayers from the prayer book that I mostly didn't understand.

At eighty-three, Dad still loves to talk about church life, especially now that I'm involved in church work. Hearing God's call to ordained ministry so early in his life means he's been actively serving God for more than six decades. He has entered into a holy time of observance and reflection that not everyone lives to see. Of course, I called him to ask him about the Lord's Prayer.

"Let's start with Our," he said. Our acknowledges our shared connectedness to our Creator. We are all children of God and when we pray to Our Father, we honor each other as siblings of the One who loved us into being.

Dad thinks the reason why this prayer has lasted so long is the phrase Our Father. This is a prayer that we pray together, even when we say it alone. We call on the God who is God to all who believe and all who don't. Our Father is simultaneously intimate and collective, as we subjugate ourselves to the position of a child, trusting in God's care. This can help heal some of the wounds you may carry if your relationship with your own father leaned closer to nightmarish than amazing. *Always remember...you have God.*

Most Saturday mornings at my house meant chores and gospel music. Andraé Crouch, Aretha Franklin, and Larnelle Harris sang to me about a Jesus who was a friend and confidant, a savior and close companion. Scripture text served as lyrics or inspiration, so while Jesus was a familiar friend, God was a strong deliverer, perfect provider, and protective shelter.

Your own father might have fallen short in offering you a deep and unfailing love, but God the Father loves you like the best possible father you can imagine—the one you want and need, who never leaves, and always, always loves you. By opening the Lord's Prayer this way, Jesus reminds us that God is not just his father, but our father, and that he's not only our father, but our Father whose Name is holiest of all holy names.

God dreamed and bore each of us into the world, and we belong to God. Our Father. Now, I don't claim to feel the same familiarity and closeness to God that I feel with my dad. Jesus leaves no room for doubt when he tells us to pray to our Father in heaven. I realize that some earthly fathers have died and are at rest in the hope of glory, so Jesus adds another qualifying phrase to eliminate all doubt about the God to whom we should pray.

Hallowed be your Name

Words mattered at my house, and the Ten Commandments were not to be taken lightly. My brothers and I faced steep penalties for speaking disrespectfully to any adult—especially my parents. The way they defended each other is a blueprint for my parenting. My siblings and I had no time to breathe after slipping up and mumbling some snide side comment before the other parent unleashed a corrective reminder about how they weren't having that disrespect. And if they were alone at the time, the other parent chastised us later.

My dad corrected us on words and phrases, helping us to understand and keep the commandments. When we stumbled with the word "hallowed," my dad explained that it meant special and holy. Both of my parents maintained a zero-tolerance policy with any form of slander or ugly talk that they referred to as "calling someone out of their name."

Words matter. Names matter even more. Growing up, I was fascinated by names and the stories behind them. My name comes from my two godmothers, Miriam Hamblin and Gwendolyn Goldsby. Perhaps I grew to love names so much because my parents loved and respected my godmothers so much that they made me their namesake. When I worked as a shelver in the library, I read books of baby names, devouring them the way you'd read a novel. I found a blank hardcover notebook and made my own book of names, organized in alphabetical order by gender, and including origin and meaning. My three girls' names came from that book—and a few of their pets' names too.

How do you feel when someone says your name? Do you feel differently when a friend or family member says it? As I investigate the myriad names for God, it is clear that God has many names, each one representing a different attribute of God.

The second chapter of Joel reminds us of this multifaceted nature of God. The chapter begins with Joel speaking of the coming day of the LORD. Over and over again, the LORD God Almighty offers a path to return to right relationship.

When Jesus teaches the disciples to pray, he begins with Our Father. When Jesus speaks to his father, he does not call to Almighty God, ruler of all people in heaven and earth. Jesus calls on his father, the One who gives him life and with whom he has a close relationship. Just before his betrayal, Jesus prays to God at Gethsemane. Realizing his death is imminent, an anguished Jesus prays using the most intimate and personal name for God—Abba. Daddy, Papa, Baba, Da, Pops, Pa. Jesus calls out to his father with the ultimate term of endearment.

The name of God that we choose when we pray matters. In the Old Testament, we have many names from which to choose to suit our petition. Healing God, Strong God, Faithful God—we can pray with any or all of these names. The name Jesus tells us to use in prayer is Our Father, our creator. When

Jesus teaches the disciples to pray, he invites them to call God their father, too. Jesus extends that same invitation to us. Doing this cements our sibling relationship with Jesus and to each other.

When my girls were little, my mom bought them an audio cassette tape called *God's Top 10*. She bought three copies: one for her car, one for my dad's car, and one for us at home. She made sure my girls had a cassette player of their own to play it on. We all sang along to "God's name is holy, God's name is holy! God's name is holy, holy is his name!" Thanks to her, my girls understand that God's name is holy, even though they live in a time and a culture where God's name isn't treated as holy.

Living in a secular society where we disrespect God's name without thinking—from casual language (Jeez) and texts (OMG) to more direct profanity—makes it easy to transgress God's rules. In this prayer, Jesus reminds us how we should treat the name of our Father each time we say it. "Hallowed be thy name" has been forgotten. When people say Jesus Christ or OMG all the time, I don't think they truly realize what they're saying. We need to remember that God's name is holy. We have this intimacy and closeness with God, but it's not mundane or banal or everyday or casual. We must address God with the respect of a parent.

Focusing on the first two lines of the Lord's Prayer redirects our attention to the similarities and differences between our relationship with God and our relationships with our parents. Not all of us have good relationships with our parents for a variety of reasons, and that's nothing to take lightly. My mom and I had a fraught relationship during my teenage years, for many typical and a few not-so-typical reasons.

Our relationship with God might give us a framework for how we long to see our parents. When our parents don't live up to our expectations, it can affect how we relate to God. One of the reasons that this prayer can be healing is because, in it, Jesus and God the Father are showing us the example of beloved child and loving parent in an open, honest, and gracious relationship. If your dad called you names, wasn't present, didn't talk to you, didn't like you, or did things that caused you even deeper pain—it can be profoundly difficult to refer to God as Father. All his life, Jesus is aware that he will have to die. He teaches, preaches, and heals knowing this hard, bare fact: death is coming for him, and it's probably going to hurt a lot. For love of us, Jesus accepts the silence of his father. And for love of the Son, the Father refuses to let death win, refuses to let the holy Name of God be disrespected, and asserts the wide breadth of I AM into the awful silence of Good Friday. Thinking about this should make us want to work harder to always treat God's name the way we do when we pray the Lord's Prayer.

Dad and I were both English majors in college. We love books, learning, and most of all, words. When I was a kid growing up with him as my priest, his sermons didn't always make sense.

But I remember that he loved to teach through his sermons, explaining the nuances of particular words and phrases in scripture. I vividly remember one statement my dad made, "To the Hebrews, holiness is a big deal. The whole idea of the Ten Commandments and all of the do's and don'ts in Leviticus is that if the Hebrews were God's chosen people, if God was supremely holy and he called the Hebrews to be holy, they had to follow certain rules."

Every generation looks at young people as rebellious rulebreakers. In my life as a parent, teacher, and youth minister—as an African American woman—I encounter extremely respectful young people and unbelievably disrespectful older adults. When I pray, I aspire to pray for both sets of people with the same level of love.

The Lord's Prayer can help us with our civil discourse, inviting us to think more deeply about how we talk to each other and being as thoughtful in addressing our neighbors as we are in addressing God. When we cultivate an awareness of how we use God's name, think of God, and regard God—with an attitude of holiness —we will be better equipped to deal with those made in the image of God, God's precious and beloved children, our brothers and sisters.

Talking about the Lord's Prayer with my father taught me a couple of things. First, just as my dad did more than forty-five years ago, this is the right prayer for parents to teach their children to memorize. It is the right prayer to pray when our own words won't come, and even when they will. Second, it taught me that I will do anything for my father, no matter how I feel about him in any given moment.

He and Mom taught me what it means to respect your parents, whether I wanted to or not. They taught me to respect God and encouraged me to want that above all things. I learned at a very early age how to listen for God's response to my prayers, because my parents taught me that listening was a sign of respect.

They also taught and modeled to me God's abiding love: no matter what we do, no matter how far we stray from God's commandments and rules, we are invited to return. "Rend your hearts, not your clothes," God says. *Don't destroy your clothing in my name; destroy your heart. Fast. Cry. Return to me with all your hearts.* Everyone gets a chance to return to God, who awaits our return with open arms, like a father.

We strive to be children of God, chosen by God, and to seek God in each other. When we pray, we pray to our Father in heaven and to the Holy Spirit who resides in each of us. Our Father in heaven who loved us into being hears us and delights in our call. Our salvation rests in the Father and is facilitated by our brother Jesus, who teaches us to pray: *Our Father in heaven. Hallowed be your name.*

CHAPTER 2

This World Is Not My Home

The Word of the Lord

Then the LORD God said, "See, the man has become like one of us, knowing good and evil; and now, he might reach out his hand and take also from the tree of life, and eat, and live forever"—therefore the LORD God sent him forth from the garden of Eden, to till the ground from which he was taken. He drove out the man; and at the east of the garden of Eden he placed the cherubim, and a sword flaming and turning to guard the way to the tree of life.

—Genesis 3:22-24

[Jesus said,] "You have heard that it was said, 'You shall love your neighbor and hate your enemy.' But I say to you, Love your enemies and pray for those who persecute you, so that you may be children of your Father in heaven; for he makes his sun rise on the evil and on the good, and sends rain on the righteous and the unrighteous. For if you love those who love you, what reward do you have? Do not even the tax collectors do the same? And if you greet only your brothers and sisters, what more are you doing than others? Do not even the Gentiles do the same? Be perfect, therefore, as your heavenly Father is perfect."

—Matthew 5:43-48

[Jesus said,] "Do not let your hearts be troubled. Believe in God, believe also in me. In my Father's house there are many dwelling places. If it were not so, would I have told you that I go to prepare a place for you? And if I go and prepare a place for you, I will come again and take you to myself, so that where I am, there you may be also. And you know the way to the place where I am going." Thomas said to him, "Lord, we do not know where you are going. How can we know the way?" Jesus said to him, "I am the way, and the truth, and the life. No one comes to the Father except through me. If you know me, you will know my Father also. From now on you do know him and have seen him."

—John 14:1-7

Your kingdom come

James Derkits

Where we are from

I found myself in East Texas at my parents' home when I began writing for this project. I picked up my father's Bible, and as I read through the readings at the beginning of this chapter, I relished the moment. My parents gave me my faith, but it has changed and evolved as I have grown into adulthood.

I sat and took notes, using the Bible they use for daily prayer. Their practice of prayer has most certainly shaped who I have become. In my formative years, I knew them to be churchgoers and volunteers in our community. I was deeply aware that they shared a regular prayer life. These practices provided for me a model of Christian life, even as my journey toward and with Jesus was becoming my own.

There I was, in their home, a place both familiar and foreign to me now. I lived in that house for a time, but I have been away from it longer than I lived there. It will always be where I am from, yet like the Garden of Eden, it is a place I can never fully return to—not like it was before, not like how I was before. And so, I came back to my home, opened my own Bible at my own desk, and continued working.

I would argue that our memories do us a favor by sentimentalizing certain parts and fogging others. The part of my childhood I remember most is running free through the tall pines, playing games with others or exploring them alone. I would take my dog and build a fort from fallen branches or amble along the creek beds.

One time I got lost and wandered for what felt like a long time until I found a house I had never seen before, even though it was actually not far from my home. Though I felt lost, I was still safe. I guess the neighborhood forest of my childhood was a lot like the Garden of Eden for me—a safe place to roam and explore and come to know God's presence. I don't know that I called it God's presence until I started going to church camp and associated the expansiveness and otherness of nature with my understanding of God.

Other memories from childhood are made up of family meals, holidays, and going to church together. I learned to be an acolyte as soon as I was old enough. One of our priests always told two jokes at the beginning of his sermon, and after that I zoned out until everyone stood for the Nicene Creed. I was confirmed in my teenage years. I remember the confirmation class lesson about grace. We each received a gift on that day. It was no one's birthday, we didn't earn it, and we didn't have to pay anyone back. We all just got a free gift. Mine was a ball that I no longer have, but I still carry the memory of it. I take out the memory when I think or teach about grace.

Not everyone lives a pleasant childhood like mine. For some, innocence ends much earlier and the memories are not nearly as Edenic. I am grateful for the woods I roamed, the family meals, and even the sermons I tuned out. These seeds of faith were planted in me and began to grow something new.

I grew up. My sexuality awakened, and my interests expanded. I wanted to be more deeply connected with others emotionally and physically. I had girlfriends and made mistakes. I got bad grades and paid the consequences. I went to church camp and met new friends. I went to college. The world of childhood came to a close. I got better grades and managed to accumulate enough hours to graduate. I met Laura, and we married, setting off on an adventure for which there is never a map. We learned about trust and forgiveness and love.

I got a job and learned a little bit about managing money. My faith expanded, and I learned how to hold the gift of doubt. This helped my childhood faith break open and begin growing into an adult faith. It taught me to let go of certain images of God and to trust instead in the mystery of God. This was not a quick discovery like Adam and Eve in the garden and their confrontation with God, naked and ashamed. Nevertheless, I was ushered out of the garden of my innocence and into the journey of an adult faith—an adult trust in God.

I prefer to use "trust" partly because "faith" has so many connotations (a particular religion or denomination or loyalty to an institution) and "belief" tends to send people on tangents about doctrine and dogma. The Greek word *pistos* is translated as all three English words: faith, belief, trust. Trust, to me, is about relationship. It also implies a willingness to follow and entrust my life to something beyond myself.

I trust God. My trust in God has come through a number of deserts of wonder and wandering. I may wrestle with doctrine and dogma, and I may look to a variety of religions and denominations to expand my understanding of my experience of God. I have mourned the death of my personal image of God, only to discover God to be more—always more—than I ever expected or could imagine.

This idea was impossible for me to conceive or comprehend as a young acolyte trying to remember when to pour water over the priest's hands or standing to hear the gospel proclaimed. Those early years were about learning from others: I was an unconscious sponge, marinating in the mystery of the liturgy and wondering what Mom brought for the potluck.

Although I can revel in the innocence of my childhood, I know that time moves forward, and I don't really want to go back. My life experiences have made me who I am in this present moment. Even if I did truly want to return to that place where God was clearly depicted in my storybook Bible and adults had everything under control, the entrance is blocked. In the Genesis story, Adam and Eve may not return to the place of their beginning. An angel stands guard with a fiery sword blocking the entrance.

But they are not sent away naked and empty-handed to figure it out on their own. Adam and Eve are given the protection they will need to survive in a dangerous world. I know I've been given what I need, even as I am still discovering and learning about the gifts I've been given. I trust that God is with me and has equipped me to face the challenges that help me discover who I am, to celebrate the joy that life brings, receive love from others, and even to trudge through the heartbreak of losing loved ones. I've been given the grace of God and the anointing of the Holy Spirit in baptism; I have been initiated into the Body of Christ, so I know I am not traveling alone.

The expulsion from the Garden of Eden equipped us. I thank God for Eve's bravery, tasting that fruit of the tree of knowledge. The reality of death and awareness of death makes life all the more precious. At the serpent's suggestion, she tasted the fruit and shared it with Adam, and our eyes were opened. There's no going back. Now we know about the wider world, and we are sent into it equipped to grow and learn.

The tension of the present

My young adulthood was spent being rebellious and daring just enough not to get kicked out of church. As I learned about scripture, liturgy, mission, and social justice for myself—even with some outstanding mentors—I sometimes thought I knew better than the church that was still forming me. Even as a newly ordained priest, I sometimes thought I was being especially clever in my sermonizing and research, only to hear the lessons of the final hymn go well beyond where I considered the daring place my sermon had landed. I learned humility, slowly.

My struggle, my rebellion, was with the tension between the world I lived in and the teachings of Jesus. I noticed and experienced a tension between two realities. They didn't match up. Jesus teaches us to love enemies, and we carpet bomb even a perceived threat. Jesus feeds people, and we live without much thought to the food deserts that sit next to centers of unimaginable material wealth. Jesus moves the ancient laws of external relationships into a spiritual, internal space, and we celebrate violence and turn sex into a commodity and marketing device. These worldly examples left me profoundly disillusioned and deeply aware of my idealism.

I remember coming home from my first mission trip in Honduras. I was leading a youth group from Houston, Texas, and we worked hard in the summer heat to build homes. We played and ate together at night, while reflecting on the day's work. I witnessed the joy of a church beating at the heart of the community where we stayed and served. Then I returned home from that week of serving people existing in crushing poverty, and I was overwhelmed by the width of our highways and the stunning array of options in the cereal aisle at the grocery store.

My learning continued in seminary. My fellow students and I bumped against one another, learned to read Greek, and developed our own theologies with insight from our church ancestors. Patient professors welcomed and helped us learn to think theologically. I worked at our library, and I remember having trouble shelving books because I wanted to read most of them. I sought understanding. Our seminary was not far from the seat of our national government. There was that kind of power, and there was the power I learned about in my New Testament class.

The kingdom of God, I learned, is not a tangible place I can visit like Washington, D.C., and it has no boundaries like the United States of America. It is not restricted to any denomination. The kingdom of God is near, and we can catch glimpses of it in worship and fellowship, in prayer and friendship. It is expressed in liberation from bondage and in agape love. This is the same love Christ demonstrates with his life and through his death and resurrection. It is a love that empowers us to become who God created us to be, giving us back our fullest, freest selves. The kingdom of God can be anywhere and with anyone. We sometimes stumble into it accidentally—but we also often arrive at it intentionally through discipline and practice.

I have dwelt in the kingdom of God in Honduras, Houston, Alexandria, and now in Port Aransas, Texas, where I serve a congregation. I have entered its gates with thanksgiving while surfing or celebrating eucharist on the beach. I probably lived in the kingdom of God longest after Hurricane Harvey ripped my town apart in 2017. In those first days, weeks, and months following the hurricane, our church opened its doors. We didn't have the answers or money or legal authority, but the Holy Spirit moved on, around, and through us. We opened our doors and began to say "yes" to the presence of the kingdom of God.

We prayed and prayed and prayed. Miracles happened through human beings showing up and material and financial donations made to our church and community. The energy of Hurricane Harvey was destructive, but it also blew a generative energy right through us. It brought us together and helped us rebuild—often better than before. The generosity shown by neighbors and strangers revealed that the kingdom of God was indeed at work among us, and we were blessed citizens of abundance.

The kingdom of God does not care that there is a disconnect between the teachings of Jesus and the world in which we live. It seems to wait patiently for an opening and reveals itself. It does not care what denomination we call home—it is our trust in God that helps us open the door. Our religious practices do not dictate where and when the kingdom will be proclaimed and seen, but opening our mouths to receive the bread of heaven shapes our lives to hunger for the kingdom's presence in the midst of life.

I still experience the disconnect between the teachings of Jesus and the world around us, even in the church. When I pray now, I try to open my heart to God. I ask for guidance in noticing where the kingdom of God is already at work around me. I seek to join in the effort. I mess up a lot. The disconnects I see in the world are probably partially reflected in the disconnects between my own life and actions and the life and actions into which I am called. There will always be that tension, and it is not mine to solve. But it is part of my job to learn to live well and joyfully in the midst of it. The practice of watching for the kingdom of God helps me to be ready whenever and wherever it is revealed.

Where we are going

Praying "your kingdom come" reorients our perspective. It admits that the coming of God's kingdom is not ours to possess or control, but God's. Praying "your kingdom come" pays homage to a reign above and beyond any earthly authority. It acknowledges God's sovereignty in the present, wherever and whenever we might find ourselves. "Your kingdom come" sets us in right relationship, as citizens and servants of God's reign. It invites God's reign right into the midst of where we are in the present moment. *Your reign, God, whatever it might entail, I desire it right here and now.*

When I think of the presence of God and the already-not-yet nature of the kingdom of God, I tend to prefer the language of the Holy Spirit. In Greek, the Spirit is feminine: *pneuma*. She shows up wherever she cares to. I can remember the first time I really thought about the Holy Spirit: a camp director brought wind surfers to a summer session to teach us about the line from John's Gospel, "The wind blows where it wills." We learned (or tried to learn) how to hold the sail to capture the wind, which would then move us. If we didn't pay attention to what the wind was doing, we would not move and would likely wear ourselves out struggling. The underlying lesson was to be aware that the Holy Spirit will do what the Holy Spirit will do, and we would do well to pay attention to her. She does what she wants. She shows up in surprising places.

Whenever we pray "your kingdom come," we should keep one eye open. The Holy Spirit is already moving. Our job is to pay attention to where she is working and try to keep up.

As often as we hear teachings about God's reign, about the kingdom of God between us, and how we have received God's grace, I worry that we are still bumbling along trying to prove our worth to God. Or maybe we are actually trying to appease that angel and sneak back into the garden (remember, there's no going back). Instead, what if we accept the gift of love God gives us again and again? What if we accept the forgiveness we have been given and stand up as forgiven and resurrected people? The world and our lives would look different if we trusted what we proclaim, and we lived as if it were really so.

When we pray "your kingdom come," we are aligning our imaginations with God's, opening our hearts to welcome the coming of that kingdom into our lives, to become the good soil Jesus is seeking. Our imaginations may be one of the most unique gifts of being human. I don't believe this was lost back in the garden, but we may have been so ashamed that we pushed it away.

Imagining God's reign and seeking to align our agenda with God's may be the most transformative action we can take. We have the ability to read the gospels, especially the parables of the kingdom, and then imagine them coming to life in the world around us. Jesus promises that the Holy Spirit will be our Advocate and that God's peace will be with us.

Practicing trust is transformative. Praying "your kingdom come" flies in the face of the disconnect between the world and the teachings of scripture. It says, *No matter how bad things seem to be, God's reign cannot be overthrown. Now what's our next step?*

There is room, we are told, in God's kingdom for all of us. Jesus has already gone ahead and is preparing a dwelling place for us. So, what are we waiting for? Imagine dwelling in that kingdom right now, in this moment we've been given—today, in this troubled world, with the people around us, and in the church.

Your kingdom come

When we invite the coming of the kingdom in the Lord's Prayer, we seek to boldly step into the reality God has prepared for us. Praying this prayer initiates a process that happens over a lifetime. Many have found the spiritual journey to be much more like a spiral than a line. We should expect to find ourselves leaving the Garden of Eden again and again and to awaken to the tension between Jesus's teaching and the world in which we live again and again. We will forget or grow lazy with our practices of trusting God and inviting the Holy Spirit to be our guide. And when we do, we can return, and pray anew: *your kingdom come.*

CHAPTER 3

The Bravest Words

The Word of the Lord

See, I have set before you today life and prosperity, death and adversity. If you obey the commandments of the LORD your God that I am commanding you today, by loving the LORD your God, walking in his ways, and observing his commandments, decrees, and ordinances, then you shall live and become numerous, and the LORD your God will bless you in the land that you are entering to possess. But if your heart turns away and you do not hear, but are led astray to bow down to other gods and serve them, I declare to you today that you shall perish; you shall not live long in the land that you are crossing the Jordan to enter and possess. I call heaven and earth to witness against you today that I have set before you life and death, blessings and curses. Choose life so that you and your descendants may live, loving the LORD your God, obeying him, and holding fast to him; for that means life to you and length of days, so that you may live in the land that the LORD swore to give to your ancestors, to Abraham, to Isaac, and to Jacob.

—Deuteronomy 30:15-20

And Hezekiah prayed before the LORD , and said: "O LORD the God of Israel, who are enthroned above the cherubim, you are God, you alone, of all the kingdoms of the earth; you have made heaven and earth. Incline your ear, O LORD, and hear; open your eyes O LORD, and see; hear the words of Sennacherib, which he has sent to mock the living God. Truly, O LORD, the kings of Assyria have laid waste the nations and their lands, and have hurled their gods into the fire, though they were no gods but the work of human hands—wood and stone—and so they were destroyed. So now, O LORD our God, save us, I pray you, from his hand, so that all the kingdoms of the earth may know that you, O LORD, are God alone."

—2 Kings 19:15-19

The earth is the LORD'S *and all that is in it, the world and all who dwell therein. For it is he who founded it upon the seas and made it firm upon the rivers of the deep.*

—Psalm 24:1-2

[And Mary said,] "My soul magnifies the Lord and my spirit rejoices in God my Savior, for he has looked with favor on the lowliness of his servant. Surely, from now on all generations will call me blessed; for the Mighty One has done great things for me, and holy is his name. His mercy is for those who fear him from generation to generation. He has shown strength with his arm; he has scattered the proud in the thoughts of their hearts. He has brought down the powerful from their thrones, and lifted up the lowly; he has filled the hungry with good things, and sent the rich away empty. He has helped his servant Israel, in remembrance of his mercy, according to the promise he made to our ancestors, to Abraham and to his descendants forever."

—Luke 1:46-55

Your will be done, on earth as in heaven

Sandra Montes

Your will be done

When my son was around four years old, he would ask everyone, "Are you mine?" It was so important for him to know that people belonged to him or that he belonged to them—that they were connected. Maybe this question was because his dad and I had separated. Maybe, like most children with their possessions, he wanted to be clear about what was his. Maybe it was because he needed assurance that he was not alone. Maybe it was because he loved the phrase, "Are you mine?" Regardless of his motivation, it made me smile every time I heard him ask. And the people he asked would smile and say, "Yes, Ellis, of course I'm yours!"

I also want people, places, and things to be mine. I want what I want. Some might say that I am set in my ways. Although I love sharing with others, people who truly know me would agree that I don't like to share what I love—especially if there is a limited supply. For example, I love Diet Coke. If there is only one Diet Coke in the fridge, you best believe and understand that it is mine.

I love thinking that God doesn't mind if I take God's last Diet Coke—that God would actually ask me to take it, would be delighted to share with me, would revel in my joy in drinking it. I am sure of that. I am sure that God is often thinking of us, favoring us in ways we don't even see or feel but that influence us mightily. The Bible declares that God will provide for all our needs and that we ought not be anxious about anything because we are valued by and valuable to God.

The Bible invites us to ask for what we want, because God wants to give it to us; to seek the desires of our hearts, so that God can fulfill them; to knock at the door, because God wants to abide with us.

Si Dios quiere is something we *gente Latina* say often. "If God wants" or "If God wills it." Sometimes we joke about it. As in, "Hope to see you in church tomorrow." "*Si Dios quiere.*" I often say, *Dios quiere*, but it depends on you—if you want. It is easier to think things happen because God wants them to happen than to say that we are following our own will.

How do we know God's will? I ask myself this all the time, not because I don't think I have a good relationship with God but because I often fear that I am not listening intently enough or that I am trying to hear God tell me that my will is also God's. For years, I have been asking God to close doors instead of opening them. I ask God to help me see God's will by closing the doors I mustn't go through. God understands that I am often distracted by too many options, and I am especially distracted by attractive options that may sound fun but may not be God's will.

Your will, not mine, be done

I say these words, and I pray that I mean them. I have noticed and learned that doing God's will is always best. I have seen that waiting for God's timing is always best, but it is tough to be patient. Recently, I felt a longing in my spirit. I felt like a change was coming in my career. I felt it palpably. Although I fought it, I applied to three different positions.

One of the places I was excited about did not offer me an interview. One of the ones I was only marginally interested in gave me an interview, but I did not get the position. I was grateful for that. And the one position I felt was made for me gave me an interview but did not offer me the position. I felt deflated, small, invisible, and discarded.

I wondered if I wasn't listening correctly to God. I prayed, and I tried to listen. I was asked to apply for a position soon after, and I said, "Unless I am definitely getting the position, I will not apply because I am burned out from getting rejected." So, I did not apply.

I sat and waited, certain that something was going to change but with no idea what. A few weeks later, I was on the phone with the president of Union Seminary, who offered me the position of interim director of worship. I felt God smiling at me and saying, "You asked for doors to be closed. My will was for this door to be open." It was a time of much rejoicing and gratefulness because God's will for my life at this time—and, truly all the time—is better than the dreams or hopes I've dared to have.

Over and over in the Bible, we read about God's will for our lives: prosperity, life, a future, hope. God's will is for us to have everything we need. God's will is for us to follow God, and to love ourselves and others. God's will is for us to take God's gifts and share them with others. We can find all of these hopes and holy aspirations throughout the Bible, including in the Lord's Prayer. We can try to understand and live God's will. We can never fully know the will of God. But we can take the time to study God's Word and spend time in quiet reflection listening intently to God's voice. I know God also speaks to us through people, situations, dreams, and visions. I am grateful because God does not give up even when I try to.

When I move out of the way, like I did with my job search, God's will is made manifest in my life. I sometimes try to help God out and, well…the results are not great. I end up hurting others and hurting myself, and things stop making much sense. For God's will to be done, I must wait and accept what is in front of me. I may not understand it, may not like it, may not agree with it, but I know I must honor it. That is one of the hardest parts for me.

Scripture offers us lessons in waiting and accepting God's will. Just think about Mary, engaged at a young age and not having known Joseph intimately. I can imagine Mary excited about her future with the man she loved (at least, I hope Mary loved Joseph). I wonder if she had decided how many children she hoped to have. I wonder if she had names picked out—and then Gabriel threw that list into chaos. I wonder if Mary was nervous about being a wife.

I remember when I was engaged to be married the first time. I remember all the excitement because I was madly in love with my now ex-husband. I wonder what Mary felt when the angel burst her bubble and told her she was going to have a child, out of wedlock.

I know many women who have gotten pregnant without being married. Some of them were extremely excited to learn the news. Some of them didn't know what to do. Some of them made very difficult decisions and choices. Some of them were extremely scared and sad. What will people think of me? What will my parents say? What will my lover say? Difficult questions, all of them. Mary's situation was different because it was God's command. And Mary said yes, even though she may have been scared or wondered what this would mean for her life—not the life of the world, but for her own singular and unique life. But I am encouraged because the Bible says that she pondered all these things, treasuring even the hard realities in her heart.

What about Abraham and Sarah? Imagine being 90 years old and longing to have a child and not being able to conceive. Then imagine your response when told that you would bear a child, even at this advanced age. Ultimately, when Abraham and Sarah accepted God's will and invited unseen angels in, they received the gift of a son, Isaac. Having a baby you have longed for and have been praying for is, undoubtedly, an amazing gift. Having a baby after you thought you were too old is a miracle. I don't know what I would have done or how I would have responded, but I believe that it is God's will to give us a hope and a future, even when we cannot see beyond our own tears.

As we follow the lineage of Abraham and Sarah in the Old Testament, we discover Joseph, their great-grandson. Joseph was a sweet, happy, precocious little brother who was favored and babied by his father Jacob and whose own mother, Rachel, struggled with the consequences of trying to help God do God's job. Well, of course the rest of Jacob's children resented Joseph. But can you imagine having the will of God exert itself on your own life, in spite of treachery and meanness?

Joseph was not only beat bloody, thrown in a hole, and sold to a caravan of passing traders, but his brothers also told their father that Joseph, his favorite, had been killed. Then, even after Joseph had worked for some wealthy, powerful people and had begun to enjoy some of life's good things, he was thrown into jail because someone lied about him. Miraculously, through the power of the will of God, Joseph was exalted and became Pharaoh's righthand man. This favor and position allowed him to save his family—the family God promised to Abraham and Sarah, and brought into being through Isaac and Rebecca, through Jacob and Leah and Rachel—from starvation and ruin. One of my favorite verses in the Bible is from Joseph's story: "Even though you intended to do harm to me, God intended it for good" (Genesis 50:20a). What a beautiful end to a life of trying to do God's will, even if it was unknown. Imagine being faithful and hopeful throughout such a life. I don't know if I could be, but I'm trying every day.

It's easy for me to forget that this world is just my temporary home. I don't think about heaven often. Sometimes, I forget to remember that Jesus and God and all the saints who have gone before me are making a space for me and that I will do the same when it is my time to die.

Instead I am usually thinking about what is happening here on earth. I sometimes wonder what God's will is for the earth itself. I am deeply concerned that we have messed up God's will for *Pachamama*—a Quechua word for Mother Earth. I don't think God expected us to make so much waste and to discard so much of it in the oceans. I don't think God's will for the earth includes my using so many single-use plastics. I don't think God's will for the earth is that we kill animals for sport or cut down trees to make room for places for our possessions. Instead, I think God's will for *Pachamama* is for us to enjoy and love and honor her. God's will for *Pachamama* is for us to be faithful and defend her, even when it is unpopular or difficult. I know that God's will for *Pachamama* is to be renewed and restored.

God's will for the earth is for us to be good stewards of creation. However, when I say these words during a service, I am often not paying attention to what this truly means. I pray for God's will to be done on earth, yet I continue to act as though I am the only one who matters. I pray these words so often, memorized in both English and Spanish, and yet I keep asking: what do they truly mean?

"Your will be done on earth" would be so different if I lived like I believed that this is not the end but rather a time to prepare for eternity, our permanent home. Does that mean I should not worry about this home? Of course not. As a matter of fact, I think we should think of this home as a rental—as a place we are holding for people who will come after us—and treat it as precious.

I think that for God's will to be done on earth, all of God's children and creatures need to coexist in peace. For God's will to be done on earth, all of us must come together and work for the common good—especially for those who need us to show up and be their voice.

On earth as in heaven

Heaven. When I think of heaven, I imagine beautiful clouds and angels busying around. I wonder if we are going to know each other like we do on earth, or if we will simply feel "connected." I wonder if there will be houses and crowns and thrones and milk and honey. I wonder if we will be reunited with loved ones who have gone before us. Will we recognize each other instantly or will it take some time? I wonder if heaven is a place where we will all be one and feel like one, not noticing anything that is different but yet somehow all our differences will be celebrated. I wonder if heaven is a place where nobody will be considered better or worse than anyone else and where we will all love being with Jesus and each other above all else.

I venture to say that God's will in heaven is expressed differently than God's will on earth. I can imagine the angels and the great cloud of witnesses are interested in only doing God's will. Nothing distracts or impedes God's will being done. In the Bible, we read different depictions of heaven and the angels who are ceaselessly praising and serving God.

On earth, we often do God's will when we want to—and even then, sometimes we do it begrudgingly. Angels, we read in the Book of Revelation, are serving before the throne of God day and night. And while they are serving God, they are praising God. Their work is prayer, and they never stop.

Few of us show that kind of reverence for God, one that is not fake or forced but a reverence of heart, body, and mind. Sometimes I catch myself thinking of other things while I'm trying to pray or read and listen to God's word. Isaiah tells us that the heavenly host calls out "Holy, holy, holy is the LORD Almighty" (Isaiah 6:3), as they reverently cover themselves before God. I wonder what it would take for me to give God that kind of selfless reverence—the kind of adoration and love that only God merits. I wonder if this is what it means to love God above everything, to embrace a profound and deep reverence that reminds me God is worthy to be praised at all times.

Oh, that I would be like the exotic and holy beasts in Revelation, who rest not day or night, singing the names of God. I wonder what my life would be like if I lived with this attitude in my mind, body, and spirit instead of wondering what to cook or who to see or what to wear. Oftentimes, the newest episode of my favorite Netflix series is longer than my prayer time. I have actually started timing myself when reading the Bible or when praying to see what one, three, five, or even ten minutes feels like. Oddly enough, when I am engrossed in a show, an hour passes, and I am just as interested and wide awake as when I started watching. What would it feel like if God's will happening in heaven—that unwavering, never-ending praise and reverence—happened on earth? What would it be like if it happened in my own heart?

As I sit and read the words again, "Your will be done, on earth as in heaven," I can't help but be confronted by the enormity of this prayer. This request is about God, not about me. As I read about the angels obeying God and praising God incessantly, I can't help but feel ashamed because I know that I don't do the same. I am also reminded that my entire being needs to be pointing to God's will in my life, not clouded with my own desires. There is a saying in Spanish—*el hombre propone y Dios dispone:* Man proposes, and God disposes. I may make a lot of plans and have lots of goals, but as a Christian I must remember that my life, my career, my relationships, and everything else are in God's hands. And God's hands are far better than anyone else's, including my own. May I ever seek to embody the words of this prayer in mind, body, and spirit: *Your will be done, on earth as in heaven.*

CHAPTER 4

Bread of Angels

The Word of the Lord

Then Moses said to Aaron, "Say to the whole congregation of the Israelites, 'Draw near to the LORD, for he has heard your complaining.'" And as Aaron spoke to the whole congregation of the Israelites, they looked toward the wilderness, and the glory of the LORD appeared in the cloud. The LORD spoke to Moses and said, "I have heard the complaining of the Israelites; say to them, 'At twilight you shall eat meat, and in the morning you shall have your fill of bread; then you shall know that I am the LORD, your God.'"

In the evening quails came up and covered the camp; and in the morning there was a layer of dew around the camp. When the layer of dew lifted, there on the surface of the wilderness was a fine flaky substance, as fine as frost on the ground. When the Israelites saw it, they said to one another, "What is it?" For they did not know what it was.

Moses said to them, "It is the bread that the LORD has given you to eat. This is what the LORD has commanded: 'Gather as much of it as each of you needs, an omer to a person according to the number of persons, all providing for those in their own tents.'" The Israelites did so, some gathering more, some less. But when they measured it with an omer, those who gathered much has nothing left over, and those who gathered little had not shortage; they gathered as much as each of them needed.

—Exodus 16:9-18

Then Jesus said to them, "Very truly, I tell you, it was not Moses who gave you the bread from heaven, but it is my Father who gives you the true bread from heaven. For the bread of God is that which comes down from heaven and gives life to the world." They said to him, "Sir, give us this bread always." Jesus said to them "I am the bread of life. Whoever comes to me will never be hungry, and whoever believes in me will never be thirsty.

So Jesus said to them, "Very truly, I tell you, unless you eat the flesh of the Son of Man and drink his blood, you have no life in you. Those who eat my flesh and drink my blood have eternal life, and I will raise them up on the last day; for my flesh is true food and my blood is true drink. Those who eat my flesh and drink my blood abide in me, and I in them. Just as the living Father sent me, and I live because of the Father, so whoever eats me will live because of me. This is the bread that came down from heaven, not like that which your ancestors ate, and they died. But the one who eats this bread will live forever." He said these things while he was teaching in the synagogue in Capernaum.

—John 6:32-35, 53-59

Give us today our daily bread

Elizabeth DeRuff

Sustenance from generation to generation

If we go back far enough, most of us can trace our heritage to people who farmed. My parents were raised in the Midwest during the Depression and World War II. This left them with an indelible imprint of thrift, mindfulness never to waste, and a deep sense of community. For my father, raised just outside of Detroit, Sundays meant church followed by lunch on Grandpa's farm in Iona. At home, their house was surrounded by a neighborhood Victory Garden. My father had a love-hate relationship with the garden. I can still hear him describing the mouthwatering taste of just-picked sweet corn. He and his brother would pick, shuck, and run ears to their mother as she stood over the pot of boiling water. It was hard, hard work. These experiences stuck with him and, to the very end of his life, he never wasted food. My father was, perhaps, the most enthusiastic leftover eater ever.

In Cincinnati, where my mother grew up, her grandfather lived close by and was an imposing, dominant figure. In my childhood home, there is a large, formal oil painting of him with an expression that makes me think I might have been afraid of him as a child. He was a judge, serving the juvenile court system and focused on social justice. Through his leadership, the court came to be known for its innovation and strong community partnerships. Pa, as he was called, started his life as a farmer. Coming from meager birth to become a respected court official made his story intriguing. I reasoned that his innovative impulses might have arisen from the oft-told story that he was frequently seen driving the horse-drawn plow with law books on his lap.

In one generation, my parents went from knowing what it meant to live off the land and close to their families to serving TV dinners to their own growing family four states away from "home." Mine was a generation of convenience foods and grandparents I only saw for a few weeks every summer. I thought Parmesan cheese came in tall green cans from the supermarket. Yet some embedded farmer-DNA must have been expressed in my genes, making me fall in love with picking tomatoes and cucumbers with my beloved grandfather during my summers in Cincinnati. There was what Koreans call "hand-taste" to these foods. Biting into a bright red orb, I could taste the joy of being with my grandfather alongside the abundant flavor of a vine-ripened tomato. These were very different from the tomatoes we ate at home: the hard, pink trios in a row, girded by white plastic wicker, wrapped in crinkly cellophane, and secured by a green rubber band, hardly tasting of anything.

Matter matters

For many city dwellers today, it seems almost impossible to understand being part of a generation for whom one pat of butter was cause for celebration, whose hands were calloused from farm implements, and whose backs were sore from the hard labor of cultivating the land and growing food. The farmers who came before us lived close to the sustenance God had given them. Their food was sometimes in short supply, yet when they sat down at the table, there was no shortage of gratitude—for the food, the Maker of the food and, undoubtedly, for the fact that the day's labor was done.

Far too many of us have lost any sense of familiarity or closeness to the food we eat and quite possibly the sense of gratitude for having food at all. The industrial food and farm system is so large and opaque that we simply don't see where our food is grown, how it's processed, or how it arrives on our store shelves. For the most part, we don't know the farmers who grow our food—or pretty much anyone else who is responsible for supplying our food. We have come to see food as a commodity always available rather than a variety of seasonal crops produced through a series of relationships: farmer, butcher, baker, consumer. Our daily bread appears so readily we don't give its abundance much thought.

Losing touch with the land, farming practices, and our farmers has dulled our senses and distorted our decision-making about food. We choose among fruits and vegetables that look picture perfect: apples that are large (sometimes so large, they look creepy), uniform, brightly colored, unblemished, and shiny. Yet these typical store-bought, perfect-looking apples don't compare in taste and nutrition to the old heirloom varieties. Our apple tree, the grandmother

Gravenstein, produces an abundance of delicious, uniquely shaped fruit in our front yard.

Worse still, scientific research points to the fact that these picture-perfect, commoditized fruits deliver only a fraction of the vitamins and minerals that heritage varieties (most especially those organically grown) apples do. These grocery story specimens look like apples, but they are lacking in full, bright flavor and nutrition. This forces us to buy synthetic supplements to make up for the lack of micronutrients in our food. When we sit down to eat, we are more likely to remember the snazzy store display than the fact that our food was once rooted to a specific piece of earth. Much of the packaging propagandizes images of cute barns and happy animals, but these images are largely fabricated.

The agents of industrial factory farming defend these practices, citing the need to feed the world. But this is also fabricated. We already grow more than enough food to feed the world. Hunger throughout the world is caused by other factors such as environmental degradation, unjust distribution, war, and food waste.

Our lack of connection cuts both ways. Most large-scale farmers don't know who's eating their crops. This isn't their fault; it's the fault of a system so elaborate that the complexity and vastness of competing global interests has made it almost impossible for producer and consumer to know each other. Farmers are paid to grow food as a commodity. You might say we are losing the forest for the trees.

The complex industries that separate farmer and eater create some unfortunate unintended consequences. At the simplest level, we aren't being fully nourished, nor do we have a say in how our food is raised, or even to observe the process. For example, if you or I raise hens for eggs or meat, we wouldn't put them into cages so small that they can barely stand up. Yet, this is the reality of modern industrial chicken ranching. Sadly and painfully, even with the designation cage-free, these poor hens don't generally see the light of day.

Our food and farm systems are based on a mechanistic model, meaning that our food is grown, processed, and delivered using an industrial process much like car assembly. Farmers aren't rewarded for growing healthy and delicious food or for treating their animals with respect. Rather, farmers and farms are rewarded for efficiency and profitability. These have become the key drivers of farming, no matter how this affects the land, animals, or our food. But the natural world—us included—cannot be assembled and taken apart like a machine. This clash, the mechanistic model overlaid on a living system, is causing harm on many different levels.

In his book *Hallowed Harvests*, Richard Scheuerman points out that these mechanistic systems do not reflect biblical mandates to recognize that the earth is holy and belongs to God (Psalm 24:1), to cultivate the land responsibly (Genesis 2:15), and to share the fruits of the earth with the poor (Leviticus 23). Industrial farming causes us to forget that the earth is alive, deeply interdependent, and flowing with

God's creative love. In his poem "How to be a Poet," Wendell Berry says that there are no unsacred places, "only sacred and desecrated places."

What does it mean to desecrate something? In part, I think it means to view an animal or plant in a utilitarian way, as separate, as some thing to be maximized, a thing that is grown and sold in such a way that the drive for profits blinds us to its interrelated nature—blinds us to its sacred reality. Industrial farming practices extraction, taking but not giving back. Jesus came to bestow life, and any system that compromises or destroys life is a system of desecration.

It doesn't take much extrapolation to realize the same mechanistic model is having an influence on us, and more than just on our physical health and nutrition. As the dominant narrative, it affects our spirituality and our relationship with Jesus, with each other, and with the earth.

Jesus understood the relationship between food and faith. One cannot read about the life of Jesus without the constant reminder that he spent a lot of his time eating and drinking, just like we do. There are many examples: the feeding of the five thousand, water turned into wine at a wedding in Cana, sitting at a table with Zacchaeus the tax collector, and eating fish cooked on the beach,

Ancient people lived close to the land. As agrarian cultures grew and developed, they saw nourishment growing in the form of grain, right outside their villages. Slaughterhouses and the business they did were not discreetly located in another neighborhood or town. The people could see and hear their meat, especially in the springtime when the baby lambs called out for their mothers. Jesus and his contemporaries understood their utter dependence upon their local food systems for life. There was no refrigeration, no supermarkets, no Amazon. If a field of crops died for lack of rain, from pest or war, people perished. Every crop and animal was precious and valued; waste was seen as dishonoring God because food is a gift from God.

Of all the foods our ancient farmer relatives harvested and produced—lentils, olive oil, fruit, dried dates and figs, goat cheese, fish and wild greens—bread was the most significant. Wheat was important and valuable because it was relatively easy to grow and easy to store. It is native to the Fertile Crescent, so it grows well in a rich soil and arid climate. Yet unlike many other foods, wheat can be stored after harvest, only becoming perishable when milled into flour.

A well-known story about the power of protecting our food supply is told in Genesis. After being sold into slavery, Joseph is brought before Pharaoh to interpret Pharaoh's dream: "I saw in my dream seven ears of grain, full and good, growing on one stalk, and seven ears, withered, thin, and blighted by the east wind, sprouting after them; and the thin ears swallowed up the seven good ears" (Genesis 41:22b-24a). God instructs Joseph to interpret the dream for the Pharaoh. He tells Pharaoh that there will be seven years of abundance followed by seven years of famine. Believing Joseph, Pharaoh collects storehouses of grain during the first seven years of plenty in preparation for the following years of famine. This turns out well for the Egyptians: "All the world came to Joseph in Egypt to buy grain, because the famine became severe throughout the world" (Genesis 41:57). Perhaps this is one of the world's oldest recorded stories about food security. It is certainly one of the most important in our own faith tradition.

In addition to wheat's shelf-life, at that time in history, it also offered a nearly perfect nutritional package providing protein, vitamins, minerals, healthy fats, and fiber—all essential for sustaining healthy, growing, resilient human lives. Living on bread and water at that time was a reasonable way to live.

Bread was also a food common to rich and poor. The biblical practice of gleaning in the harvested wheat fields made it possible for even the poorest to eat. Leviticus 23 guided the farming practices of the children of Israel, "When you reap the harvest of your land, you shall not reap to the very edges of your field, or gather the gleanings of your harvest; you shall leave them for the poor and for the alien" (verse 22).

Given its relative ease of growing, storage, nutritional value, and accessibility to rich and poor alike, bread was the most ordinary and basic food that united all people of the ancient Middle East. This is still true in some cultures today. Bread is so important that the Egyptian word for it is *Aeesh*, which also means "life." From this wheat-saturated context, Jesus proclaimed, "I am the bread of life" (John 6:35). This announcement was obvious and needed no further explanation for Jesus's followers. What they would have heard and understood is that Jesus was as essential to them spiritually as bread was to them physically. Just as our physical bodies need food to survive, our spiritual selves need nourishment, too.

On the night before Jesus died, he ate a meal with his disciples. He asked them—and us—to remember him each time we share bread and drink wine. He said, "Take, eat, this is my body which is given for you, do this in remembrance of me." The phrase "in remembrance of me" is significant. To my knowledge it is the only time Jesus ever asked his disciples to remember him. By contrast, Jesus, over the course of his ministry, bids those whom he has healed to tell no one and repeatedly directs worship and praise to his Father. Why would he ask us, in this tender moment, to remember him?

Jesus's instruction to remember him is as important for us today as it was for the disciples. Jesus became incarnate. He became matter, and all matter is suffused with God's creative spirit. When we eat bread, it becomes part of us. When we eat the bread that is the Body of Christ, we literally incorporate Jesus into our bodies, reminding us of our union with him and with all of creation.

On a biological level, wheat is a grass arising from the earth that essentially enables us to eat sunlight. Wheat plants use the energy of the sun, combined with water and carbon dioxide, plus nutrients in the soil to create carbon sugars and oxygen, all through the process of photosynthesis. But what happens in the soil is the real variable in the process. In healthy farming systems, the carbon sugars created through photosynthesis are shuttled down through the roots of the plant where an elegant exchange occurs underground between the plant and the surrounding soil microbes.

Here on a subterranean level, the plant exchanges carbon sugars for nutrients produced by the surrounding soil-dwelling microbes. There's quite a party going on down there! This mutually beneficial relationship is essential for producing nutrient-rich plants and keeping our soil healthy. When we eat bread, especially bread made from wheat grown using organic practices, our bodies utilize the atomic elements of the plant—carbon, nitrogen, phosphorus, etc.—as the building blocks for every cell in our body.

I love the Jewish blessing over bread that expresses this elegant cooperation so poetically: "Blessed are you, Lord God, King of the Universe, who brings forth bread from the earth." The image of bread rising from the earth by the will and grace of God reminds us that a wheat field is as much a part of the Body of Christ as the consecrated bread on our altars.

Maybe it's been a while since you've eaten bread, or maybe you had some for breakfast. Regardless, the physical symbol Jesus left for us no longer means what it did to his disciples. Whether it's because of low-carb diets or gluten concerns, bread has become so diminished and demonized that it no longer symbolizes the food necessary for life. How can we understand that Jesus is essential to our lives if the symbol he used points to a food many avoid or shun?

The bread Jesus shared with his disciples is different from the bread we eat today. Bread has changed—and not for the better. We settle for wheat that's grown on fields sprayed with chemicals that make God's earth and creatures sick. We settle for bread made from flour that is so white and over-processed, it has only a fraction of the nutrients it did when Jesus ate it. It's no wonder that people have challenges digesting it.

If we tested our communion bread in a lab, would we find the life-giving quality to which Jesus compared himself? Would we find chemicals like glyphosate? Would we perceive the lack or the presence of "hand-taste?" This sounds obvious, but how we treat wheat and flour is manifest in our sacraments. The idea of bread being life-giving and calling it the Bread of Life is for the most part a theological maxim but no longer a biological truth. And this is a problem of the body and the soul.

God's fidelity and our response

Most scientists agree that we can link all wheat to a grain called Einkorn, the grandmother of all wheat, found in the Fertile Crescent. In ancient times, seeds like Einkorn and other naturally adapted varietals were carried literally all over the world. In each location over time, the seeds took on the character of the place, the *terroir* (a French word, akin to the idea of "hand-taste" that indicates the literal flavor of the soil in a particular locality), and became what scientists call "landrace."

Peasant farmers and indigenous people have long been the custodians of these seeds, knowledge, and land husbandry. They understand the preciousness of each part of the cycle. Wheat seeds are passed down from generation to generation. Some spend long periods in seed libraries. Some end up forgotten in dusty Mason jars, knit with lacy cobwebs on the shelves of old barns. More recently, some seeds are genetically patented by giant multinational corporations that own the rights to their actual DNA and forbid farmers from replanting them. This practice forces farmers to purchase new seeds each year, rather than saving seed from their crops—a radical change in farming traditions that are as old as civilization. While there are more than 140,000 different varieties of wheat held in the world's seed banks, only a fraction of that number is commercially farmed due to the emphasis solely on yield.

During the spring of 2019, I organized a small group to plant four rare varieties of heirloom wheat, the types that Jesus would have eaten. One of these varieties comes from Israel. In his book *The Triumph of Seeds*, Thor Hanson tells the fascinating story of the discovery of one of these varieties of wheat. On top of a 1,000-foot rock cliff, overlooking the Dead Sea, is a natural rugged fortress called Masada. The only route up was a steep, winding trail known ominously as the snake path. The Roman general Flavius Silva and an enormous legion of soldiers arrived at the base of Masada in the winter of 72-73 CE. His legion had direct orders from Rome to crush the community of insurgents living in the fortress. These people were Jewish extremists, called the Sicarii, who were the last survivors of the widespread uprising known as the Great Revolt.

Despite the treacherous terrain, General Silva was victorious and infiltrated the fortress. Rather than surrender, risk capture, or worse, nearly 1,000 Sicarii men, women, and children committed suicide. Before they died, not wanting the

Romans to claim anything of value, they moved everything in their storehouses into a central warehouse. Then they set the building on fire. The wooden rafters and stone walls crumbled inward, creating a heap of ash and stone that remained untouched for nearly 2,000 years.

In *The Jewish War*, the historian Josephus, in 75 CE, describes what was contained in these storehouses: "Wheat in plenty was laid up, ample for the needs of the beleaguered for a long time, and wine and oil in abundance, as well, all sorts of pulses and dates heaped up together."

In the 1960s, the Israeli archeologist, Dr. Yigael Yadin, translator of the Dead Sea Scrolls, discovered the Masada store of salt, grain, olive oil, wine, preserved dates…and wheat. The excellent preservation of these foods was possible because of the extremely arid climate and the mass of ash and stone from the fire covering the storehouse contents, preventing oxidation. Remarkably, flesh still clung to a Judean date. The wheat seeds were still viable. The wheat found at Masada is called Hourani. Some of these seeds traveled to the USDA seed bank in Aberdeen, Idaho, then on to the principal plant breeder, Steve Lyon, at Washington State University Bread Lab. Anyone can order seeds, even Hourani, from the USDA. They send five grams of seed which, translated into wheat, means about forty seeds. These forty seeds were propagated, partly with my project in mind. Steve surprised me with a small plastic bag of approximately 14,000 seeds, descendants from his own original forty Hourani. Receiving these rare kernels as a gift gave me profound pleasure to be part of saving something so small, and yet so significant.

We plant wheat in the Russian River Valley in Northern California, where the soil is fertile and the climate favorable. The soil needs to be soft and free of weeds and rocks. A small piece of equipment we use for planting is called a Seedway, which looks like a simple, non-motorized lawn mower. The sower pushes the Seedway, filled with the selected seeds, and it first makes a shallow furrow and then disperses the seeds neatly in a row at a set interval. We use several Seedways and are careful to plant each variety: Sonora, Karun, Tamilka, and the Hourani in distinct areas.

When it comes time to plant the Hourani, I ask permission of the others to be the one to sow them in the earth. Taking the plastic bag filled with ancient and heroic heritage of holy food thrills me. Hourani seeds are very small, the size of a grain of rice but shorter and more round on the ends. They are a creamy, rich, dirty-blond color with a crease bisecting one side, top to bottom. I sense that the seeds are eager, almost hungry, for the earth, waiting to practice their ancient art of germination, rooting, and pushing up toward the sunlight. The last step is to roll a heavy compaction-roller across the field, compressing the seeds firmly into the earth for a strong seed-to-soil connection. We then wait for rain.

In the fullness of time, a trio of field-side musicians inspire a large group of community volunteers who gaily harvest our crop by hand with sharp sickles. Once fully cleaned, the Sonora is stone-milled into flour and baked into communion bread. Since we have far less of them, the harvested seeds from the other three types will be replanted in order to cultivate a greater abundance of those varieties for future eating.

After the harvest, we thresh. Threshing removes the seeds from the seed head. We borrow an old green and red bundle thresher where one person feeds a sheaf of wheat, head side down into the rapidly rotating wheel, whacking the seeds loose. These fall into a small tray at the bottom. The result is pretty messy because there's a lot of chaff as well as stems that get through along with the seeds. Winnowing is the next process, and it's how we separate the wheat from the chaff.

Tiny tan bits of chaff adorn my straw hat and stick to my sweaty blue cotton shirt and skin as they fly off the thresher. As I stand in my dusty brown leather boots in the parking lot of the farm, it is at least 100 degrees. I'm taxed but also elated. In my hand I'm holding a white nylon sandbag with a self-tie. On the bag I've written, "Honoré Farm and Mill 2019, Hourani." This bag weighs five precious pounds, all harvested from the small plastic bag we started with in March. In this bag is a tangible link to history and identity, to our Jewish forefathers and mothers who struggled against oppression and for freedom and cultural continuity in the face of forces that sought to erase them. In a few months, we'll replant the seed and God willing and weather permitting, we'll harvest enough grain next August to actually stone-mill some Hourani into flour and bake it into communion bread. Once milled and baked into bread, I'll taste for the first time and at long last the courage of the Sicarii. I'll taste my friend Steve's foresight and generosity. And I'll taste our fidelity to the grain, this amazing gift we have been given.

Fidelity to the grain means standing in the long, long line of farmers who have been saving, exchanging, and breeding seeds for millennia. Fidelity to the grain means being mindful of the way we farm these seeds—only using regenerative organic or biodynamic practices to work with what our siblings in the Andes call *Pachamama* rather than against her. It means milling the grain in such a way that nothing is wasted—and that the food made from these grains is truly nourishing, delicious, and easily digestible. It means telling the stories of the grain, so that the knowledge isn't lost.

More than all of this, practicing fidelity to the grain responds to God's fidelity to us. God is loyal to us even when we are not. God's undying fidelity to us is the ground upon which we can stand and make our lives. Therefore, our fidelity to the grain—indeed to the entirety of the natural world—is a way that we can imitate God.

I stand in this lineage of farmers who have saved seeds, anticipating and praying for an abundant harvest, and enduring the years when crops fail with hope and confidence in God's fidelity toward us and all of Creation. The joy of this reality is secured in my heart, right next to my love for my grandfather. And this daily bread and holy nourishment is where food and faith and land and love become one. *Give us this day our daily bread.*

CHAPTER 5

Seventy-Seven Times

The Word of the Lord

The LORD spoke to Moses, saying: Now, the tenth day of this seventh month is the day of atonement; it shall be a holy convocation for you: you shall deny yourselves and present the LORD'S offering by fire; and you shall do no work during that entire day; for it is a day of atonement, to make atonement on your behalf before the LORD your God. For anyone who does not practice self-denial during that entire day shall be cut off from the people. And anyone who does any work during that entire day, such a one I will destroy from the midst of the people. You shall do no work: it is a statute forever throughout your generations in all your settlements. It shall be to you a sabbath of complete rest, and you shall deny yourselves; on the ninth day of the month at evening, from evening to evening you shall keep your sabbath.

—Leviticus 23:26-32

Then Peter came and said to him, "Lord, if another member of the church sins against me, how often should I forgive? As many as seven times?" Jesus said to him, "Not seven times, but, I tell you, seventy-seven times.

—Matthew 18:21-22

From noon on, darkness came over the whole land until three in the afternoon. And about three o'clock Jesus cried with a loud voice, "Eli, Eli, lema sabachthani?" that is, "my God, my God, why have you forsaken me?" When some of the bystanders heard it, they said, "This man is calling for Elijah." At once, one of them ran and got a sponge, filled it with sour wine, put it on a stick, and gave it to him to drink. But the others said, "Wait, let us see whether Elijah will come to save him." Then Jesus cried again with a loud voice and breathed his last. At that moment the curtain of the temple was torn in two, from top to bottom. The earth shook, and the rocks were split. The tombs also were opened, and many bodies of the saints who had fallen asleep were raised. After his resurrection they came out of the tombs and entered the holy city and appeared to many.

—Matthew 27:45-53

Forgive us our sins as we forgive those who sin against us

Ryan Black

"Wash me through and through from my wickedness and cleanse me from my sin... wash me, and I shall be clean indeed."

—Psalm 51: 2, 8b

I never wanted to get to know the God of the Old Testament. Quite frankly, that God was someone I was afraid to know. He seemed awfully hard to please. He was the referee watching my every move, waiting for my foul, ready to throw the flag at the first sign of infraction or imperfection. He was the stern disciplinarian, the authoritarian parent with impossible standards, the teacher who had predetermined that I was not an A student. His standards were high, and his judgment was swift.

After all, this was the God who had thrown Adam and Eve out of the Garden of Eden for eating a piece of fruit. I was certain I had committed larger infractions, and thus spent much of my early childhood imagining being cast out of my mother's backyard garden. I imagined being led through the chain-link fence and having the gates locked behind me. There I would stand in the dirt-and-gravel alley, on the outskirts of our yard and my mother's love, watching as my more righteous and obedient older sisters laughed and played on the swing set in the yard from which I'd just been banished. Forever.

I grew up in church, so it goes without saying that I had also been introduced to the God of the New Testament, the God who became incarnate, suffered death, was buried, and was resurrected on the third day—all to save me from original sin. I knew that this was a good thing, that the scary God had reconciled himself with creation through this very big, very complicated act. Would this God open the back gate and allow me back in the yard? Would this God have tossed me out into the alley in the first place?

A part of my five-year-old self could imagine this other version of God like an old, wise grandparent, arms always outstretched and waiting to give me a hug and five dollars. But another part of me wasn't so sure. The idea of God having God's son sacrificed (in what the crucifix hanging above the altar at my home parish portrayed to be a very gruesome manner) seemed another red flag that vengeance was the ultimate name of God's game.

My family was very faithful and very regular in our attendance at church and church functions, but I was full of doubts at an early age. It wasn't that I questioned God's existence but rather that I doubted my own abilities to navigate these complicated issues under the watchful eye of a God who didn't seem to put up with any nonsense. Even as a child, I knew I was well acquainted with nonsense. While age brought with it clarity for many of life's mysteries, I have to admit that I remained pretty puzzled about God, particularly when my middle school classmates raised in evangelical traditions started talking about their personal relationships with God.

Personal relationships? How exactly was that supposed to work? To have a relationship, you must approach a person, and I was still feeling like I'd be cast into the back alley at any moment for saying the wrong thing to Old Testament God. It certainly didn't help that around this time I began to realize that there was something about me that was very different from other young boys my age. For me, included within the suite of awkward realizations puberty brings with it, I harbored a growing understanding that I was gay.

If there was one thing I knew for sure about being gay, it was that my parents could never forgive me for being this way. I could never forgive myself for being this way. And God, who tossed out Adam and Eve for an unauthorized snack, would certainly never, ever forgive me for being this way.

And so it was settled: I would cope. I would become the ideal Christian. I would attend Mass each Sunday and also before catechism classes on Wednesday nights. I would join the church youth group. I would go the extra mile and join the youth groups of other churches in town, as well. And any time I had any thoughts about my sexuality or anything remotely related to it, I'd pray or read the Bible or simply turn off the part of my brain so eager to acknowledge this authentic self that was bubbling to the surface. I would keep my hands constantly busy to prevent them from becoming the devil's tools. And it worked. For a time, anyway.

Near the end of my first semester in college, my carefully curated system of suppression and mechanical movement failed.

It didn't happen in bits and pieces as these stories often do, but all at once, as I sat in the university chapel listening to a homily. The campus priest reminded us that God's forgiveness was conditional upon our willingness to repent, to turn our backs on sin, to chart a new path of righteousness. It wasn't enough that Christ died for our sins if we weren't also successfully obtaining and actualizing religious perfection. God was disappointed in us if we weren't doing this, the priest professed. At the time, I saw this sermon—what I call the Forgiveness Homily—as a fatal moment, one that triggered my complete undoing. It was the end of everything I'd known and professed all my life, the turning of my back on God, creed, and family. I was an apostate. My life as I had known it had ended.

I would later come to respect that dreadful moment after the Forgiveness Homily as the one in which my relationship with God truly began. It was also the moment in which I realized everything I had ever thought about forgiveness was completely wrong. What happened after the Forgiveness Homily was unprecedented for me in my short time on earth: I left Mass before the eucharistic prayer began. It would be years before I would return. I applied and transferred to a larger university where I knew fewer people and where the ones I did know could be avoided. I came out to myself by writing the words, "I am gay," in my journal. I found a therapist and made it a point to be on time to every appointment. I got a job and began banking a nest egg in case my parents cut me off when I came out to them. I made new friends—backup friends (I thought) who could step in when others abandoned me.

A foreign feeling emerged. I was happy—happy and sustained for the first time in my life. Buoyed by that hope, I began coming out to others—first to a handful of trusted childhood friends, then to my sisters, and finally to my parents. At almost every turn, the conversations went about as I had expected them to—worse than I had hoped, but predictable. With few exceptions, most people reacted to the news with surprise and hostility. A few friends and family members turned their backs. "Your house is burning down," an older family friend wrote to me after she'd heard about my coming out through the small-town grapevine. "Ask the Lord for forgiveness immediately. And your poor parents! Ask them for forgiveness too."

Needing to seek forgiveness for being myself was a concept I couldn't grasp. And so, I rejected the people in my life who thought that was what I needed to do. In many cases, I raced them to the rejection line. And off I went to build my new life, embracing my newly discovered authenticity. There was joy in becoming acquainted with my genuine self. There was also heartbreak over the loss of my loved ones. I was simultaneously free and imprisoned, not by a secret I was burying deep inside but by the loss I felt by no longer keeping it.

"Have you considered what it would look like to forgive your parents?" a university therapist asked during one of our sessions. I was stoic.

"No. They haven't asked for it. They don't think they're wrong."

"Do they need to?" the therapist asked, curiosity in her voice.

Suddenly I was cast out into the alley again. I rattled off my own Forgiveness Homily. "Forgiveness is reserved for those who realize they were wrong, who repent, who choose a new path. They haven't done any of those things. They don't care. They don't even want forgiveness."

Reasonably, you could say I had some hang-ups—some of which I still have today. In fact, one of my hang-ups is about being seen as the Prodigal Son. I was certain with every fiber of my being that my parents were the Prodigals, and I was also certain that as soon as they learned the errors of their ways, I would be standing at the end of the road, hands outstretched magnanimously, ready to forgive them. I fantasized about how this would play out, ruminating when I had trouble sleeping at night about how poetic it would feel to receive an apology.

"I am ready to forgive them as soon as they come asking," I told my therapist. I'd repeatedly spoken of my religious upbringing by that point in our relationship, and my therapist was well aware that my worldview was largely grounded in the Bible and a faith-focused upbringing, despite my current status as an apostate. That day I left therapy with an assignment to collect "evidence" that the formula for forgiveness I'd articulated— that an apology was a precursor to every act of forgiveness—was the correct one. Specifically, I was to look for biblical evidence that this was the case. I was asked to get to know that unapproachable Old Testament God. I did not complete that assignment before my next appointment. In fact, I didn't complete it for more than a decade.

Life went on for me, as it tends to do. I graduated and moved away from my home state. I began a master's program at a liberal college in the Northeast and got a job that rewarded hard work with reasonable money. I loved the predictability of this life, and I began to date. I found more opportunities to give or withhold forgiveness there. Life was fine.

Life was fine, absent the large hole where my family would have been. By this time, we were all back on speaking terms and discovered plenty of safe topics to keep us from addressing the elephant in the room. We had found our process, our way of relating and keeping the right distance. My parents loved the sinner but hated the sin. But I could not separate them from their sins or infractions. I could not love them at the same time that I despised their failure to acknowledge who I was. And so, we did it all over again—my finding opportunities to remind them that I was gay, their reacting by withdrawing and withholding affection, affirmation, and attention. There would be months of silence, and eventually there would be a thawing and a reunion of some sort. But there was never forgiveness or reconciliation in any true sense of the word in this season of our life together. There was simply frustration, withdrawal, exhaustion, recovery, and reconnection.

Predictably, my college therapist was not the last person to suggest I forgive my parents. Another therapist, years into my adulthood, encouraged me to do so and to explore the underlying biblical framework through which I'd based my beliefs on forgiveness. By this time, I was living in San Francisco and had visited many of the churches in town, finally finding a parish focused on service to others, especially the city's significant homeless population. Something about the act of serving others softened my heart and an "aha" moment emerged. This felt like humanity to me. This felt like a place where a living and loving God might be.

For many Christians I know, the idea of a human side to God is all but foreign. But for me, this was the very essence of Jesus: God in human form, acquainted with all the pains and joys of life on earth. And Jesus had always fascinated me with his acts of love and charity, keeping company with lepers and tax collectors, and using his last words to ask God to forgive the very people who were in the process of executing him. But I'd also had a difficult time reconciling this Jesus, the Jesus of the gospels, with everything I'd heard from the pulpits of my childhood. Jesus, along with his deep humanity, had somehow gotten thrown out with the bathwater when I began to reframe my ideas of Old Testament God.

And so it was through those acts of mercy, charity, and service at my San Francisco parish that I became reacquainted with Jesus and with the God who so decisively wanted reconciliation with humankind that this God was willing to experience life as a human and have that life come to a painful end. This moment of reconnection was a moment of reconciliation all its own, between God and me. As I forgave myself for walking away, for having accepted the misguided messages of God the Punisher, I discovered my need to be forgiven for having badly misunderstood God's role in all of this in the first place—for having so badly misunderstood God's deep love for me, for all of us, for each of us.

Some fourteen years after it had first been handed to me, I set out to complete my therapist's homework assignment. I would open my Bible and attempt to determine exactly what God thought about forgiveness. I would examine my own beliefs about forgiveness, and I would accept whatever disconnect arose. I would be open and willing to retire old belief systems if I arrived at new conclusions. I would stop exiling myself in the alley. I would have a good attitude about forgiveness and forgiving and being forgiven, even if it killed me. And if it did actually kill me, I would have all of the answers I needed once I finally met Jesus.

Here is what I learned: I learned that forgiveness is such a fundamental tenet of Christianity—so central to our faith that it is discussed more than 150 times in scripture. Forgiveness is so important that God asked Moses to set aside an entire day for atonement, and by doing so, Moses and his people would be cleansed. And while there are plenty of times that Old Testament God looked to sacrificial ritual to determine a person's sincerity in asking for mercy, it struck me that Old

Testament God didn't always need to be asked before freely offering forgiveness. It struck me that Old Testament God and New Testament God might be one and the same.

God's forgiveness is enormous and timeless. Indeed, there is no greater example of forgiveness than is expressed through God becoming human, experiencing human life and then trading it, so that all of humankind could once again enjoy the promise of paradise without the sting of sin and death. There would be no one left out in the alley. There never had been an alley, anyway. I learned that it is important to God that we forgive others, not only those who acknowledge their trespasses or believe they trespassed in the first place. Forgiveness requires an unmitigated and unmerited kind of grace. Forgiveness is the bridge that spans the chasm between our hearts and Christ's—especially when our imperfect, flawed nature resurfaces. But for most of us, forgiveness does not come naturally. It is a practice, a discipline, an art, an instrument to be finely tuned and well-oiled.

In its purest form, forgiveness is limitless. Forgiveness is the opening of a cell door, letting sorrow and regret escape. It is an acknowledgement of the fear, anger, confusion, and sadness that trap and weigh us down, and it is the conscious decision we make to choose grace instead. We are all in need of others' forgiveness. And we all need to forgive ourselves.

Leviticus instructs that forgiveness cleanses; the psalmist extols its powers of purification. Forgiveness is the children of Israel putting their hope in the Lord, transforming their scarlet sins into snow-white wool. Forgiveness is an omnipotent, all-powerful, all-knowing God choosing to become forgetful about our imperfections.

But forgiveness is also a young boy who wants to please God, to please his parents, to be kept in the fold—and the boy who will fail at all of these things, lose faith in Church, doubt God's existence, suffer, fall, feel robbed of love, and withhold love from others. It is the same boy who willed himself to stop blaming God and others for his predicament, who accepted that he was doing his best all along, and stopped damning himself to hell over it.

Forgiveness is that young boy growing into a man, looking back from the middle of his life, acknowledging his regrets, and accepting that he did his best. Forgiveness was the letter from my best childhood friend, who herself had not known what to think when I told her I was attracted to men, saying nothing of the angry words we had exchanged, but only "I love you. Could we start again, please?"

Forgiveness is accepting that my family wouldn't attend my wedding because it was too much for them—and to be disappointed and sad about their choice, but appreciating that they are humans doing their best as well. Forgiveness is feeling angry about that all over again some days and starting over on the forgiving. Forgiveness is giving myself that break when I need it. More importantly, forgiveness is giving my parents that break, accepting that they may not have the capacity to accept my sexuality but knowing they are still doing their very best to love me anyway, in their own way. Forgiveness is their ability to tolerate stories about my marriage—no longer demanding my silence about this very real, very important part of me. Forgiveness is our willingness and commitment to love each other as who we are, even when it's hard and uncomfortable.

Forgiveness is my sisters, not knowing how to ask for reconciliation outright, calling to see if they can come visit and meet my husband. Forgiveness is their willingness to cast aside the shame they believe I caused our family and meet the person who means so much to me, because they know their gesture will mean so much to me too. Forgiveness is hurriedly preparing my home with fresh-cut flowers, cooking meals fit for a holiday, and picking them up at the airport when they arrive, thrilled to bring them to my home where I will introduce them to the one who is home to my heart.

Because forgiveness is loving one another. Forgiveness is love.

CHAPTER 6

Plenteous Redemption

The Word of the Lord

Out of the depths have I called to you, O LORD; LORD, hear my voice; let your ears consider well the voice of my supplication. If you, LORD, were to note what is done amiss, O LORD, who could stand? For there is forgiveness with you; therefore you shall be feared. I wait for the LORD; my soul waits for him; in his word is my hope. My soul waits for the LORD, more than watchmen for the morning, more than watchmen for the morning. O Israel, wait for the LORD, for with the LORD there is mercy; with him there is plenteous redemption, and he shall redeem Israel from all their sins.

—Psalm 130

The people who walked in darkness have seen a great light; those who lived in a land of deep darkness—on them light has shined. You have multiplied the nation, you have increased its joy; they rejoice before you as with joy at the harvest, as people exult when dividing plunder. For the yoke of their burden, and the bar across their shoulders, the rod of their oppressor, you have broken as on the day of Midian. For all the boots of the trampling warriors and all the garments rolled in blood shall be burned as fuel for the fire.

—Isaiah 9:2-5

Ahab told Jezebel all that Elijah had done, and how he had killed all the prophets with the sword. Then Jezebel sent a messenger to Elijah, saying, "So may the gods do to me, and more also, if I do not make your life like the life of one of them by this time tomorrow." Then he was afraid; he got up and fled for his life, and came to Beer-Sheba, which belongs to Judah; he left his servant there.

But he himself went a day's journey into the wilderness, and came and sat down under a solitary broom tree. He asked that he might die: "It is enough; now O LORD*, take away my life, for I am no better than my ancestors." Then he lay down under the broom tree and feel asleep. Suddenly an angel touched him and said to him, "Get up and eat." He looked, and there at his head was a cake baked on hot stones, and a jar of water. He ate and drank and lay down again. The angel of the* LORD *came a second time, touched him, and said, "Get up and eat, otherwise the journey will be too much for you," He got up, and ate and drank; then he went in the strength of that food forty days and forty nights to Horeb the mount of God. At that place he came to a cave, and spent the night there.*

Then the word of the LORD *came to him, saying, "What are you doing here, Elijah?" He answered, "I have been very zealous for the* LORD*, the God of hosts; for the Israelites have forsaken your covenant, thrown down your altars, and killed your prophets with the sword. I alone am left, and they are seeking my life, to take it away."*

He said, "Go out and stand on the mountain before the LORD, for the LORD is about to pass by." Now there was a great wind, so strong that it was splitting mountains and breaking rocks in pieces before the LORD, but the LORD was not in the wind; and after the wind an earthquake, but the LORD was not in the earthquake; and after the earthquake a fire, but the LORD was not in the fire; and after the fire a sound of sheer silence.

When Elijah heard it, he wrapped his face in his mantle and went out and stood at the entrance of the cave. Then there came a voice to him that said, "What are you doing here, Elijah?"

—1 Kings 19:1-13

I do not want you to be unaware, brothers and sisters, that our ancestors were all under the cloud, and all passed through the sea, and all were baptized into Moses in the cloud and in the sea, and all ate the same spiritual food, and all drank the same spiritual drink. For they drank from the spiritual rock that followed them, and the rock was Christ. Nevertheless, God was not pleased with most of them, and they were struck down in the wilderness.

Now these things occurred as examples for us, so that we might not desire evil as they did. Do not become idolaters as some of them did; as it is written, "The people sat down to eat and drink, and they rose up to play." We must not indulge in sexual immorality as some of them did, and twenty-three thousand fell in a single day.

We must not put Christ to the test, as some of them did, and were destroyed by serpents. And do not complain as some of them did, and were destroyed by the destroyer. These things happened to them to serve as an example, and they were written down to instruct us, on whom the ends of the ages have come. So if you think you are standing, watch out that you do not fall. No testing has overtaken you that is not common to everyone. God is faithful, and he will not let you be tested beyond your strength, but with the testing he will also provide the way out so that you may be able to endure it.

—1 Corinthians 10:1-13

Save us from the time of trial

Cohen Adkins

I had a hard time writing this chapter. When first approached to contribute to this book, I was flattered and excited to share what the Holy Spirit led me to share, and I wanted to communicate things in the most eloquent and erudite of ways. Except there was a slight hitch in my plan. When I say slight, perhaps it would be best for you to visualize "slight" as a massive iceberg, similar in size to the one that sank the unsinkable Titanic.

This iceberg, a construct of my own making, contains myriad emotions and injustices holding my soul and thoughts prisoner. It has been through the opaqueness of this emotional iceberg that I have been able to view my life and faith recently. The view through the icy walls is poor. This monster of emotion has tagged along everywhere: work, the gym, the grocery store, and unfortunately even at church.

That parishioner with the invisible chip on their shoulder sitting in the back pew? That was me. Replace the ice chip of bitterness on my shoulder with a giant iceberg of emotion. If you can see that this frozen behemoth is breaking out the stained-glass window at the back row, then you get the picture. There I sat, blocking the grace of God and the redeeming message of Christ from my mind and soul with my frostbitten heart and embittered emotions.

As summer lagged on and my submission deadline for this chapter loomed, I found myself compelled to write this essay, to share my burden—the one my spirit is compelled to wrestle with and to explore. My only theological background is secondary education in parochial schools and hours spent in church, Sunday school, and church summer camps. Nonetheless, I offer this attempt to give word to the yearnings and leanings of my soul. I hope this speaks truth and hope to you. I pray that the Holy Spirit can use the ramblings of a world-weary soul such as me to communicate a meaningful message to you.

Life is hard. I know we see much variance around the specifics of the word "hard," but lack of consensus on its definition doesn't detract from the reality of the impact of the many hard and brutal injustices of human life. Famines, wars, pandemics, political shenanigans, gang warfare, the opioid epidemic, immigration reform, terror attacks, international corporate misdeeds, climate change, millennials and their fancy avocado toast decimating the housing market. This list of injustices hardly covers the life-changing, mood-altering news stories of the past decade, let alone the last ten months, ten weeks, ten days, or ten minutes.

On both local and global scales, there seems to be no end to the misery which we humans inflict on ourselves. I imagine these trespasses, those endured and those doled out, much like a polished stone skipping across still pondwater, each point of impact creating an oscillation. These reverberations expand further and further out from the main point of impact, concentric circles spreading, disturbing the still surface. In such a way, trauma spreads. Each trespass committed in a community mars the face of the block, the neighborhood, the city.

The small town where I grew up recently made national news. Splashed across city newspapers, our tiny hamlet made the headlines. In the last few months, certain misdeeds, mishandlings, and overall negligence were brought to light. Twenty-one million missing dollars, fourteen indicted top-level local government officials, and a sheriff's suicide turned the community upside down. All of a sudden, this small mountain town went from occasional social media shout-outs during festivals and fall foliage to becoming a real-time John Grisham novel.

In the midst of the chaos of federal and state police investigations, zealous reporters swooping into town to get the scoop, and scrambling politicians eager to save face, a community languished in chaos. Maybe the more cynical and skeptical among us saw this coming. Lack of committee oversight on backroom business deals, glad-handing contract and vendor negotiations, and pork-barrel politics all intertwined and combusted, consuming themselves and leaving confusion in their wake.

"These are the times that try men's souls." I wonder if even Thomas Paine, the eighteenth-century political activist, could have imagined the current political landscape. Politics, for better or worse, shapes the lives of us all. From the hierarchies of ancient Mesopotamia to the global economic negotiations in Davos, Switzerland, politics and its influence on the composition and comportment of society have always influenced the individual. Why else would Marx have been inspired to write his manifesto or Tocqueville to pen his marvel on democracy? The state of politics in a country, town, or hamlet often influences the feelings of those who live in them. If political tensions are high and individuals experience an overarching sense of political turmoil and distrust of power, then there is no peace. A sense of unease brews.

I often want to check out from this constant tension and retire to my hermit hole or wander for forty days and nights in the desert. While this kind of retreat may be beneficial and restorative, self-imposed seclusion can only last so long. Jesus may have wandered in the desert and spent years preparing for his ministry, but eventually he had to actually do the work. He stepped out from the background and humbly began following the path that would lead him to the cross. He became, however reluctantly or unintentionally, a political figure. His ministry to the bruised and broken, the ostracized and unclean was revolutionary. He challenged the religious dogma of his community and the power structure of the Roman empire, and ultimately this led to his death.

I think we often forget the very political nature of this Christ we serve. God born into the vessel of humanness as Jesus of Nazareth became a political symbol—not a partisan symbol to be trotted out but a symbol of the politics of the kingdom of God, where there is miraculous abundance, and everyone belongs. Ultimately, through the machinations and subversion of the politics of empire, God's true purpose for humanity came to fruition. Jesus was the ultimate sacrifice, and it took the workings of an earthly empire and the maneuverings of a partisan religious sect to bring about humanity's redemption. This redemption meant the death of Christ, the breaking of his body and shedding of his blood. This act has been commemorated, celebrated, and remembered since that Last Supper. But in our own souls' commemoration and celebration of this sacrifice in Holy Communion, let us not forget the implications of our accepting such a gift.

As a child growing up in a Southern Baptist congregation, hunger pains always hit right in the midst of the morning service. If it was Communion Sunday, then the tiny swig of grape juice and one tiny wafer of bread acted as a mid-morning snack that I would consume as slowly as possible, savoring the bit of sustenance it provided. For this reason, I looked forward to Communion Sunday with great anticipation and salivation. I am not so sure that my child-self would have liked communion in the Episcopal Church. I doubt the tang of port would have held the same mid-morning appeal.

When I first began visiting the Episcopal church as a young adult, I was in awe at the thought of celebrating Holy Communion every Sunday. It was such a potent reminder of Christ's sacrifice. I quickly accepted and deeply cherished the practice of remembering and acknowledging that gift at every service—partaking of it freely, with an invitation for all to participate. In the liturgy, after the Peace, Holy Communion begins. After the Great Thanksgiving, the story of Christ's ultimate sacrifice is recounted to the congregation. We proclaim the mystery of our faith. We ask for sanctification. Then, in boldness, we recite the prayer Jesus taught to his disciples: "Our Father, who art in Heaven, hallowed be thy name..."

There is something remarkably cathartic in the repetition of this prayer. When I was a child, I memorized it for a project in Sunday school. I received a red foil star on my achievement chart, a sticker of my choice, and praise from my parents and teacher. Since my six-year-old mind first encountered these words until today, the Lord's Prayer has filled a void inside me. It seems to be the quintessential Christian prayer. If up for a vote in high school superlatives, the Lord's Prayer would surely receive "Most Popular." It is the prayer most Christians, regardless of denomination, have repeated in services and learned during formation. Matthew's account of Jesus's Sermon on the Mount include this prayer, and its inclusion in our liturgy reflects its importance and applicability to the past, present, and future.

The repetition of the Lord's Prayer, together and in harmony with myriad, distinct, and separate voices, is my favorite part of the liturgy. It is a poignant reminder of the fragility of both our faith and our human nature. Our dependence on our Heavenly Father to provide sustenance and protection, and to forgive us our sins, is clearly stated in its few short verses. This prayer, spoken first by a Savior and then repeated throughout generations by those in search of salvation, perfectly proclaims humanity's need for Jesus's redeeming and reconciling sacrifice of love.

As the congregation prays together, each individual acknowledges their dependence on God's grace and forgiveness. Each individual proclaims praise and all glory to our Creator God. As each person repeats these words, the congregation is collectively praying and praising. As each person repeats this prayer, they are both asking forgiveness for trespasses made against others and acknowledging the importance of forgiving trespasses committed against them.

In meditating on these words, in accepting this invitation to write, God used my ego to God's advantage. In reflecting on a few simple sentences, God penetrated the blocks of bitterness that had been building up like permafrost on my shoulders, blocking my mind and heart from the piercing redemptive love found in the words and work of Christ. I had allowed my fear for the future and my bitterness over institutional corporate sin on personal, local, and global levels to meld into a resentful mass. I had carried this cold fear and deep hurt with me throughout the comings and goings of my life. Every frightening news story, every recorded misdeed became another reason for my anger and resentment, another layer of ice to dull my vision. Then, Jesus Christ took a wrecking ball to my iceberg and sat me down in the lifeboat of this prayer he asks us to pray. In the words of the prayer, I was "saved from the time of trial."

When we recite the Lord's Prayer, we acknowledge the reality of God with reverence. We look to the future of the church and the world with an expectancy that God's will is being fulfilled. We ask God to provide for us and protect us from our own personal temptations and threats of evil. We ask for forgiveness of our sins, and we acknowledge the importance of giving forgiveness to others. This is the expectation Jesus has for us. This is a tenant of the faith he has taught us with his life, death, and resurrection.

My iceberg of bitterness was fueled by my own fear and self-pity and was also wrapped up in a whole lot of unforgiveness. As I contemplated the Lord's Prayer, each line and verse reverberated in my head, but one word stood out: FORGIVE. Forgive as Christ forgave. Forgive as Christ taught you. Forgive as the Lord's Prayer reminds us to at each Holy Eucharist.

Life is hard. Life was hard for Jesus, too. We cannot—we must not—allow the meanness we see in the world around us to harden our hearts or let anger drive a wedge between our Savior and our souls. We must forgive.

When we pray the Lord's Prayer together, we join our voices with the voices of Christians the world over, all expressing the same powerful message and promise of faith in our Christ. This message, this good news about a rebel from Judea—God in a human vessel—has the ability to transform the world, to change political climates, to shelter the refugee, to feed the hungry, to give sight to the blind, to raise the dead to new life, and to rescue each one of us from our self-imposed misery. God's love and promise in the form of Jesus changed the world forever. And Jesus's message, his promises, and his love have the ability to change the human soul over and over.

Let God meet you there, in the middle of the service, in the simple words of a simple prayer. Let God transform your fears into forgiveness. Let God protect you from evil and be your daily bread. And let God save us from our times of trial.

CHAPTER 7

My Refuge and My Stronghold

The Word of the Lord

He who dwells in the shelter of the Most High abides under the shadow of the Almighty. He shall say to the Lord, *"You are my refuge and my stronghold, my God in whom I put my trust." He shall deliver you from the snare of the hunter and from the deadly pestilence. He shall cover you with his pinions and you shall find refuge under his wings; his faithfulness shall be a shield and buckler. You shall not be afraid of any terror by night, nor of the arrow that flies by day. Of the plague that stalks in the darkness, nor of the sickness that lays waste at mid-day. A thousand shall fall at your side and ten thousand at your right hand, but it shall not come near you.*

Your eyes have only to behold to see the reward of the wicked. Because you have made the Lord *your refuge, and the Most High your habitation, there shall no evil happen to you, neither shall any plague come near your dwelling. For he shall give his angels charge over you, to keep you in all your ways. They shall bear you in their hands, lest you dash your foot against a stone. You shall tread upon the lion and the adder; you shall trample the young lion and the serpent under your feet.*

Because he is bound to me in love, therefore will I deliver him; I will protect him because he knows my Name. He shall call upon me, and I will answer him; I am with him in trouble; I will rescue him and bring him to honor. With long life will I satisfy him, and show him my salvation.

—Psalm 91

I am speaking the truth in Christ—I am not lying; my conscience confirms it by the Holy Spirit—I have great sorrow and unceasing anguish in my heart. For I could wish that I myself were accursed and cut off from Christ for the sake of my own people, my kindred according to the flesh. They are Israelites, and to them belong the adoption, the glory, the covenants, the giving of the law, the worship, and the promises; to them belong the patriarchs, and from them, according to the flesh, comes the Messiah, who is over all, God blessed forever. Amen.

It is not as though the word of God had failed. For not all Israelites truly belong to Israel, and not all of Abraham's children are his true descendants; but "It is through Isaac that descendants shall be named for you." This means that it is not the children of the flesh who are the children of God, but the children of the promise are counted as descendants. For this is what the promise said, "About this time I will return and Sarah shall have a son." Nor is that all; something similar happened to Rebecca when she had conceived children by one husband, our ancestor Isaac. Even before they had been born or had done anything good or bad (so that God's purpose of election might continue, not by works but by his call) she was told, "The elder shall serve the younger." As it is written,

"I have loved Jacob,but I have hated Esau."

What then are we to say? Is there injustice on God's part? By no means! For he says to Moses, "I will have mercy on whom I have mercy, and I will have compassion on whom I have compassion."

So it depends not on human will or exertion, but on God who shows mercy. For the scripture says to Pharaoh, "I have raised you up for the very purpose of showing my power in you, so that my name may be proclaimed in all the earth." So then he has mercy on whomever he chooses, and he hardens the heart of whomever he chooses.

You will say to me then, "Why then does he still find fault? For who can resist his will?" But who indeed are you, a human being, to argue with God? Will what is molded say to the one who molds it, "Why have you made me like this?" Has the potter no right over the clay, to make out of the same lump one object for special use and another for ordinary use? What if God, desiring to show his wrath and to make known his power, has endured with much patience the objects of wrath that are made for destruction; and what if he has done so in order to make known the riches of his glory for the objects of mercy, which he has prepared beforehand for glory— including us whom he has called, not from the Jews only but also from the Gentiles? As indeed he says in Hosea,

"Those who were not my people I will call 'my people,'
and her who was not beloved I will call 'beloved.'"
"And in the very place where it was said to them, 'You are not my people,' there they shall be called children of the living God."

And Isaiah cries out concerning Israel, "Though the number of the children of Israel were like the sand of the sea, only a remnant of them will be saved; for the Lord will execute his sentence on the earth quickly and decisively." And as Isaiah predicted,

"If the Lord of hosts had not left survivors to us, we would have fared like Sodom and been made like Gomorrah."

What then are we to say? Gentiles, who did not strive for righteousness, have attained it, that is, righteousness through faith; but Israel, who did strive for the righteousness that is based on the law, did not succeed in fulfilling that law. Why not? Because they did not strive for it on the basis of faith, but as if it were based on works. They have stumbled over the stumbling stone, as it is written,

"See, I am laying in Zion a stone that will make people stumble, a rock that will make them fall, and whoever believes in him will not be put to shame."

—Romans 9

Also read the Story of Gideon in Judges 6-7

And deliver us from evil

Catherine Meeks

Though we pray the bit of the Lord's Prayer that includes the words, "and deliver us from evil," we have a difficult time internalizing the words. But internalizing them helps us understand what it means to be delivered, what is involved in the process of deliverance, and the role that we must take in helping that work to be done in our hearts and minds and in our world.

In the twenty-first century, we tend to give evil either too much or too little credit. With those who think that everything bad is the result of evil or the devil, it is difficult to explain their own role in what is happening to them. But others believe evil is not alive in the world today, that everything is simply up to us.

Both of these ways of looking at life miss the point: evil is real, and we are responsible for the ways in which we invite it into personal and communal life. There is a great temptation to assign all evidence of evil demonstrated through less than righteous behavior to some outside force. If this force is perceived as some kind of energy that has moved into our lives and disrupted us individually or collectively and we call it evil, then it has the power to immobilize us. It is easy to come to the conclusion that there is nothing to do but pray because we cannot see ourselves having any power with which to address this force of evil.

Prayer is indeed crucial to our journey with God. Each and every person has been gifted with great inner resources that can be brought to our pilgrim journey on this earth. It is God's expectation that those resources be discovered by us and used to help us become the people we were sent to earth to be. We are expected to do this discovery work so that our lives will not become like the tumbleweed, blown from place to place by every wind that comes. The work of deliverance begins in the heart and soul of the pilgrim who is seeking to discover their gifts and use them along the path to healing. Deliverance shows us a way to live in peace on this earth.

Perhaps the longest journey we ever take is from the head to the heart. This is especially true for us in this post-modern era, because we have so much access to amazing power sources. It is easy to turn to money, position, or social connections in the external world, or to education and one's ability to become a wizard, viewing technology as the best source of power for any and every journey. But this way of thinking is a major hindrance to gaining access to the source of power that leads to an authentic self—toward the possibility of a life of peace grounded in a deep and true understanding of all of the corners of one's inner landscape.

Those who have read any of my work elsewhere, especially on the topic of becoming beloved community, or who have heard me speak, will quickly recognize common themes. If I am evangelistic about anything, it is that inner work has to be done—and it is the work of a lifetime. There are not any shortcuts. If this work is not done, there will be a great deficit in the person trying, and this deficit makes it difficult to be delivered from evil. It is impossible to separate evil from good when you lack self-awareness.

The work of becoming aware and awake is a process that has to be engaged in a very honest and intentional manner. At times, this process needs to be coached by others (sometimes professionals) who are capable of providing good, sound guidance. One of the ways that we might think of evil working is by reinforcing ideas that prevent us from seeking help to do our necessary, personal inner healing work.

The best example of this is the idea that a person is crazy if they seek out a therapist to help with the inner journey of healing. Nothing could be further from the truth. Reducing the distance between the heart and the mind as we search for inner healing can help to build a clearer understanding of how evil engages us in our daily lives. This type of intuitive knowledge is very helpful in the deliverance process. When we ask for deliverance but block the channels for deliverance to move through us, we are seeking something we are not prepared to receive.

In order to make this point a bit larger, I will share a short story from my own efforts to learn who lives in my inner community. I grew up in rural Arkansas with an illiterate sharecropping father and a schoolteacher mother who, because of the lack of access to higher education and the circumstances of her life, worked for eighteen years to complete her college education. My mother graduated from college the same year I graduated from high school. She had engaged a long struggle in order to reach this goal.

My household was poverty stricken. Though we had food and relatively decent housing, there were many things lacking in my early life because we simply did not have money. I learned how to do without and lower my expectations. My most vivid memory of this is the beginning of the school year and always being without proper shoes to wear. I regularly missed the first day of school. New shoes were necessary in order to go back to school. I could not figure out why my parents did not get the shoes earlier since they knew when school was to begin, but they did not.

There is nothing more exciting for a child than going to school on the first day and reconnecting with old buddies and learning what has happened during the summer. But I missed those days every year. We worked in the fields, and I wore out my shoes from the previous year. We also went barefoot a lot during the summer.

I lived for many years with a little wounded girl in my heart, a little girl who felt she could not get what she needed. It was difficult to ask people for anything later in my life because I had internalized the message of scarcity. I became accustomed to making do or doing without. In some ways, it was quite comfortable. It was not easy to allow for prosperity to be a part of my life even when it was possible. I had to work very hard in my personal healing journey to allow that inner little girl to learn that the old days were really gone and that my adult life of being empowered and economically stable was different from my parents'. Whatever was immobilizing them was not paralyzing me anymore. I had to take responsibility for stepping into a new way of being.

Often, evil energy manifests itself in our lives as a distraction. My scarcity mindset distracted me from the abundance that God intended for me. No, I wasn't mindlessly preoccupied with prosperity to the point of opulence, but I lacked a clear-headed and heart-centered acceptance of an abundant life. An abundant life sees possibilities instead of limitations. These limitations are rooted in a lack of trust in God's power to protect us from evil.

People of faith, integrity, and goodwill rarely find themselves doing evil things that are harmful to others such as exploiting children, selling drugs, stealing—or all those things that seem to result from folks turning themselves over to the forces of evil. However, it's easy to be subtly caught by evil when we are distracted. There are so many times in the day that we can lose our essential ability to be focused. This struggle is compounded by our lack of knowledge about the many selves that live in our inner communities. These dynamics come to us through the narratives in our families of origin, along with cultural narratives, and our personal experiences that bear witness to those narratives. We are a composite of all of these stories—and much more. Thus, it is imperative that we spend time becoming acquainted with those parts of ourselves that have been shaped by our experience. It is profoundly important for us to understand that we have great potential that can be accessed when we are willing to do the necessary inner work. It is neither simple nor easy to separate the unconscious parts of ourselves from the parts that we know and use to present ourselves to the world.

Unfortunately, there are too few places in our culture to help us in finding our way into this work. Our religious and educational communities place great emphases on acting correctly, which is usually defined by some set of external variables and those who have been a part of our early formative life. Of course, there is validity in having such external checks and balances, but if you are attempting to make it through the world without doing the inner work of discovering what lies at your core, it will be impossible to be the authentic person that God intends for you to become.

Courageous self-interrogation demands that we be clear about what motivates us to do the things we do and to think the thoughts we think. We need to ask hard questions about what we are thinking, how we are behaving—and listen carefully for the still, small voice of God answering us from deep in our core.

If we are not willing to engage in this process, we will continue to replay the voices of others as our guides and spend a lifetime blown around by hot air, creating a lot of conflict for us. One of the greatest losses in avoiding our own inner work is our inability to hear what God wants of us. It is in hearing and responding to God's call in our lives that we invite the healing energy of the Holy Spirit to enter into our hearts in ways that deliver us from evil.

There are things that happen to the best of us—things that do not make sense to us, even when we are doing our inner work and trying our best to hear the voice of God and to respond with all of our heart. Evil is an energy system that exists in the world and undergirds the expression of much bad behavior that can impact us regardless of our following our paths. It is true that evil visits all of us at times, but how we respond is dependent to a great extent on how we have developed our inner authentic self.

God allows us to be presented with the invitation to respond to evil. It seems that there are times when evil is granted an opportunity to disrupt people who have no right to be disrupted. There is no denying that we do not always understand what is happening in our lives (or the lives of others) when it comes to evil. We must remember that evil can be resisted at every juncture if we do our inner homework and stay awake to the life that is ours to live. We will not avoid encounters with evil, but we will handle them differently if we have done the necessary inner work. In spite of what may happen, we can find our way back to balance, because finding balance is a matter of going to the depths of our souls and finding the still place that connects us to God, the source of all peace and healing.

Our peace is not contingent on avoiding evil but is based on our remembering that God is our source and that God can be trusted to be present regardless of our circumstances. God is present whether God is called or not called. Psalm 91 tells us that God shelters us in God's wings, like a mother shelters her young. This is a very comforting thought when we truly understand that our energy is not well spent in trying to avoid whatever comes our way; that faith, inner work, and continual conversation with all of the parts of ourselves and with God will stand us in good stead no matter what happens.

Many voices in our outer world discourage us from embracing life with an attitude of deliverance. In the present moment, the voice of fear may be one of the loudest voices speaking against the faith and hope that we will be delivered from evil. Voices that call us to be afraid and give in to hopelessness have not encountered their own inner communities.

Deep fearfulness comes from not being able to imagine what it is like to confront the unknown. We doubt our ability to survive in spaces where there are unknowns, accompanied by a sense of powerlessness. We can clearly see how not knowing ourselves will make us afraid of the outer world, because so much of the way we see the outer world is mirrored by our inner world. If there is little to no conversation with our inner world, then the outer projections are laced with fear and a sense of not having control. This happens because there are simply too many unknowns for the unconscious person to navigate. The ego steps in to offer help and its best help is expressed in creating a way to make it through the world deeply rooted in fear.

Fear offers a sense of control over the unknown. The unknown is controlled in the mind of the fearful by fear itself. When we refuse to let go of the fear that nothing can be trusted and nothing will work out for us, our fears will always be rewarded. But if we let go of the fear and allow life to unfold, our lives will have energy and vitality.

Many challenges come to meet us each day. We can choose the ways we embrace them. As we face each day with the expectation of finding hopeful, healing light, we will find that light. If that light is confronted by evil, it can continue to shine because it is rooted in our deep, authentic self—the self that lives in conversation with God and cannot be extinguished by the force of evil or any other challenge.

It is important to remember that when we encounter evil, we must pay attention. There will be expressions of it that will create sadness and sorrow, distractions and distress, but the awakened human is saved by the knowledge that evil will never have the last word. No matter what happens to us—in a minute, hour, day, or lifetime—as a result of evil, it will not have the last word. Evil is in conflict with the intention of God, and God will have the last word.

Some days, it is easier to remember this good news than other days, but if we reaffirm it enough, it will come back to the forefront of our hearts, whether we are consciously trying to remember it or not. We need to practice remembering in order for this reality of God to become rooted so deeply that we are clear that nothing can separate us from the watchful eye, protective love, and grace of God. Remembering that God has the last word is crucial and practicing remembering this helps to make it possible. We must stay awake to all of the small and inconsequential times of distraction, discerning the ways in which they make us forget to stand in the faith of what we know. These pesky and petty things can cause us to slip into fear almost without our knowledge, unless we develop and practice the holy habits of self-interrogation, prayer, silence, meditation, study of scripture, and other practices that support our growth.

Recalling God's goodness in the midst of distraction and recollecting our inner selves calls us back to the place where we remember that we will be delivered from evil. Called or not called, God is present.

CHAPTER 8

Counting On

The Word of the Lord

Now when Solomon finished offering all this prayer and this plea to the Lord, he arose from facing the altar of the Lord, where he had knelt with hands outstretched toward heaven; he stood and blessed all the assembly of Israel with a loud voice:

"Blessed be the LORD, who has given rest to his people Israel according to all that he promised; not one word has failed of all his good promise, which he spoke through his servant Moses. The LORD our God be with us, as he was with our ancestors; may he not leave us or abandon us, but incline our hearts to him, to walk in all his ways, and to keep his commandments, his statutes, and his ordinances, which he commanded our ancestors. Let these words of mine, with which I pleaded before the LORD, be near to the LORD our God day and night, and may he maintain the cause of his servant and the cause of his people Israel, as each day requires; so that all the peoples of the earth may know that the LORD is God; there is no other. Therefore devote yourselves completely to the LORD our God, walking in his statutes and keeping his commandments, as at this day."

Then the king, and all Israel with him, offered sacrifice before the LORD. Solomon offered as sacrifices of well-being to the Lord twenty-two thousand oxen and one hundred twenty thousand sheep. So the king and all the people of Israel dedicated the house of the LORD. The same day the king consecrated the middle of the court that was in front of the house of the LORD; for there he offered the burnt offerings and the grain offerings and the fat pieces of the sacrifices of well-being, because the bronze altar that was before the LORD was too small to receive the burnt offerings and the grain offerings and the fat pieces of the sacrifices of well-being.

So Solomon held the festival at that time, and all Israel with him—a great assembly, people from Lebo-hamath to the Wadi of Egypt—before the LORD our God, seven days. On the eighth day he sent the people away; and they blessed the king, and went to their tents, joyful and in good spirits because of all the goodness that the LORD had shown to his servant David and to his people Israel.

—1 Kings 8:54-66

For I am about to create new heavens and a new earth; the former things shall not be remembered or come to mind. But be glad and rejoice forever in what I am creating; for I am about to create Jerusalem as a joy, and its people as a delight. I will rejoice in Jerusalem, and delight in my people; no more shall the sound of weeping be heard in it, or the cry of distress. No more shall there be in it an infant that lives but a few days, or an old person who does not live out a lifetime; for one who dies at a hundred years will be considered a youth, and one who falls short of a hundred will be considered accursed. They shall build houses and inhabit them; they shall plant vineyards and eat their fruit. They shall not build and another inhabit; they shall not plant and another eat; for like the days of a tree shall the days of my people be, and my chosen shall long enjoy the work of their hands. They shall not labor in vain, or bear children for calamity; for they shall be offspring blessed by the LORD*— and their descendants as well. Before they call I will answer, while they are yet speaking I will hear. The wolf and the lamb shall feed together, the lion shall eat straw like the ox; but the serpent—its food shall be dust! They shall not hurt or destroy on all my holy mountain, says the* LORD.

— Isaiah 65:17-25

But you, beloved, must remember the predictions of the apostles of our Lord Jesus Christ; for they said to you, "In the last time there will be scoffers, indulging their own ungodly lusts." It is these worldly people, devoid of the Spirit, who are causing divisions. But you, beloved, build yourselves up on your most holy faith; pray in the Holy Spirit; keep yourselves in the love of God; look forward to the mercy of our Lord Jesus Christ that leads to eternal life. And have mercy on some who are wavering; save others by snatching them out of the fire; and have mercy on still others with fear, hating even the tunic defiled by their bodies.

Now to him who is able to keep you from falling, and to make you stand without blemish in the presence of his glory with rejoicing, to the only God our Savior, through Jesus Christ our Lord, be glory, majesty, power, and authority, before all time and now and forever. Amen.

— Jude 1:17-25

Then I saw a new heaven and a new earth; for the first heaven and the first earth had passed away, and the sea was no more. And I saw the holy city, the new Jerusalem, coming down out of heaven from God, prepared as a bride adorned for her husband. And I heard a loud voice from the throne saying,

"See, the home of God is among mortals.
He will dwell with them as their God;
they will be his peoples,
and God himself will be with them;
he will wipe every tear from their eyes.
Death will be no more;
mourning and crying and pain will be no more,
for the first things have passed away."

And the one who was seated on the throne said, "See, I am making all things new." Also he said, "Write this, for these words are trustworthy and true." Then he said to me, "It is done! I am the Alpha and the Omega, the beginning and the end. To the thirsty I will give water as a gift from the spring of the water of life. Those who conquer will inherit these things, and I will be their God and they will be my children. But as for the cowardly, the faithless, the polluted, the murderers, the fornicators, the sorcerers, the idolaters, and all liars, their place will be in the lake that burns with fire and sulfur, which is the second death."

Then one of the seven angels who had the seven bowls full of the seven last plagues came and said to me, "Come, I will show you the bride, the wife of the Lamb." And in the spirit he carried me away to a great, high mountain and showed me the holy city Jerusalem coming down out of heaven from God. It has the glory of God and a radiance like a very rare jewel, like jasper, clear as crystal. It has a great, high wall with twelve gates, and at the gates twelve angels, and on the gates are inscribed the names of the twelve tribes of the Israelites; on the east three gates, on the north three gates, on the south three gates, and on the west three gates. And the wall of the city has twelve foundations, and on them are the twelve names of the twelve apostles of the Lamb.

The angel who talked to me had a measuring rod of gold to measure the city and its gates and walls. The city lies foursquare, its length the same as its width; and he measured the city with his rod, fifteen hundred miles; its length and width and height are equal. He also measured its wall, one hundred forty-four cubits by human measurement, which the angel was using. The wall is built of jasper, while the city is pure gold, clear as glass. The foundations of the wall of the city are adorned with every jewel; the first was jasper, the second sapphire, the third agate, the fourth emerald, the fifth onyx, the sixth carnelian, the seventh chrysolite, the eighth beryl, the ninth topaz, the tenth chrysoprase, the eleventh jacinth, the twelfth amethyst. And the twelve gates are twelve pearls, each of the gates is a single pearl, and the street of the city is pure gold, transparent as glass.

I saw no temple in the city, for its temple is the Lord God the Almighty and the Lamb. And the city has no need of sun or moon to shine on it, for the glory of God is its light, and its lamp is the Lamb. The nations will walk by its light, and the kings of the earth will bring their glory into it. Its gates will never be shut by day—and there will be no night there. People will bring into it the glory and the honor of the nations. But nothing unclean will enter it, nor anyone who practices abomination or falsehood, but only those who are written in the Lamb's book of life.

— Revelation 21

For the kingdom, the power, and the glory are yours, now and for ever. Amen.

Sam Portaro

Prayer is not an easy subject for me. One of the several bishops who have had the misfortune of responsibility for me dared to ask me about my prayer life. He did not seem amused with my answer that I didn't have a prayer life, at least not in any sense I think he'd have found orthodox. I take the Collect for Purity at its word: I believe in a God "to whom all hearts are open, all desires known, and from whom no secrets are hid." I can't tell God anything God doesn't already know.

But I also know it takes a lot of work to forge a mature relationship with God—or anyone else. Living into a relationship entails ups and down, togetherness and apartness, a host of other opposites and every subtle gradation in between. Knowing and accepting this reality is a hallmark of maturity. Knowing and accepting this reality in one's relationship with God is spiritual maturity and a grounded faith—not the pleasantly warm glow of sunset through stained glass but a robustly comforting strength like a red-hot woodstove.

I long ago abandoned any notion that my recitation of the Lord's Prayer, silently or aloud, had any influence upon God. God has other—and better—things to do than to listen to my spiritual equivalent of a robocall. But seriously grappling with the Lord's Prayer requires that I revisit it, as I have done in essays, books, sermons, classes, conversations, and now in this reflection. For this book, the portion of the prayer assigned to me is its conclusion. This is an interesting choice for many reasons, among them the fact that there's some question of whether it belongs to the whole or not.

This magisterial conclusion of the Lord's Prayer in a flourish of the impressive trinity of every human heart's secret desire—kingdom, power, and glory—appears only in certain late manuscripts of Matthew's Gospel (6:13). It follows a common Jewish practice of closing prayer with a doxology, a brief hymn of praise. Similar doxologies appear in Christian scriptures, the most similar being the closing of the epistle of Jude:

> *Now to him who is able to keep you from falling, and to make you stand without blemish in the presence of his glory with rejoicing, to the only God our Savior, through Jesus Christ our Lord, be glory, majesty, power, and authority, before all time and now and for ever. Amen.* (verses 24-25)

A version of the Lord's Prayer is found in Luke's Gospel (11:2-4) as Jesus's response to a request from one of the disciples, "Lord, teach us to pray, as John taught his disciples" (Luke 11:1). The longer form is tucked into the fourth and fifth chapters of Matthew's Gospel. These chapters gather up teachings of Jesus from many sources and contexts, placing them in a unified setting—literary license taken by the authors and editors of the gospel, much as a script writer might combine several scattered episodes of a novel into a single scene.

The Lord's Prayer is a text that resists being reduced to its parts. There's a unity to it. And like a Chinese finger puzzle, the more I pulled at it, the tighter it grew. Part of the tension was my resistance to traditional notions of prayer as words addressed to God. I do believe articulating our hearts' desires, darkness, and demons is important. But the primary importance and benefit are to me. Like words spoken aloud to a therapist, hearing ourselves saying certain things aloud is essential to our own healing and ultimately, to the healing of all creation.

So, I couldn't separate the end of the Lord's Prayer from everything that precedes it. I couldn't make it conform to a model of prayer that tradition had taught me. I was therefore required to engage it as one does a friend, entering into and reflecting on where it came from, has been, and how it came to be included in The Story at the heart of Christian faith told in the gospels.

The gospels were crafted from decades of stories about Jesus passed by word of mouth from person to person, community to community. Even after they were put in writing, rare copies of scriptures inscribed on precious scrolls were read aloud, generating commentary and conversation in cultures where literacy was reserved to a few.

Jesus lived within Jewish communities that read scriptures aloud and studied them in Hebrew but spoke Aramaic as their *lingua franca*, their common language. Aramaic was a Syrian dialect common to the region around Galilee where trade routes and politics fed cultural and linguistic diversity. As Jesus's ministry and influence spread within the relatively small geographic area he traveled, Jesus found that Jews gathered around him—and after his death, they gathered around his disciples. Curious non-Jews, Gentiles, were attracted and sought inclusion.

The story of the cross-cultural emergence of a new community that comes to call its members "Christians" is told in the Acts of the Apostles, believed to be of the period and authorship of the Gospel according to Luke. Jesus's teachings were rooted in and often referenced Jewish scripture and history. Gospels and letters from apostles who later ministered to the infant Christian communities tailored their teaching to their context. Matthew's Gospel presumes a predominantly Jewish audience familiar with these references.

Beyond the gospels, a version of the Lord's Prayer concluding with a similar ascription is found in the *Didache,* an early document dating to the first or second century that gathered up teachings of Jesus for Gentile believers. There are similarities between Matthew's Gospel and the *Didache*: each is a compilation of teachings attributed to Jesus, each is written in an informal Greek dialect, *Koine*, and both are conscious of the Jewish-Gentile division.

Fast-forward to times, technologies, and texts relevant to our present encounter with this prayer. Common access to biblical scriptures was a fundamental principle of the Protestant Reformation. Its architects and adherents maintained the right and responsibility of every person to read, study, and debate religious scriptures as essential to an informed faith. The Book of Common Prayer gave English-speaking peoples access to scriptures and devotional texts previously largely available only in Hebrew, Greek, or Latin.

But the most significant development in English was the translation of the Bible authorized by James I in 1604 and completed in 1611, thereafter known as The King James Version. In that translation, Matthew 6:13 was rendered: "And lead us not into temptation, but deliver us from evil: For thine is the kingdom, and the power, and the glory, for ever. Amen."

The inclusion of a final doxology in this landmark translation is notable, in part, for the extensive influence of the King James Version as a primary text delivered into the hands of common people just as advances in printing and education opened literacy to the masses. While the first Book of Common Prayer was published in 1549 and went through several successive editions, the extended version of the Lord's Prayer including this ascription did not appear in the Book of Common Prayer until 1662, the first edition published after the King James Version of the Bible.

The Lord's Prayer is now commonly used in worship with and without the final praise, so what difference does this addition make? What are we to make of this appended coda that lists a trinity of God's definitive assets: the kingdom, the power, and the glory?

More Than a Prayer

Developed by specific authors, editors, and communities in the first century, each gospel served specific—and separated—communities of Christians as the primary instrument of formation in the community that embraced it. Creeds documenting the basic beliefs of Christians began to emerge a full century later, the first—the Apostles' Creed—perhaps around 120-180 CE. Within the gospels and epistles, we detect the elements of early faith statements, of principles and practices taught as components of a lived faith—if I believe this, then how should I live? As its title indicates, the Lord's Prayer belongs to Jesus. It's a descriptive statement of faith in God as Jesus experienced God. It's also reflective of Jesus's own response to God in relationship.

Perceived through this lens, the Lord's Prayer becomes more than a template for personal conversation and communion with God. As one who claims kinship with Jesus as brother, who seeks to see and respond to God as Jesus does, I see the Lord's Prayer as a statement of what I believe about God—the principal correspondent in the core relationship of my life, the primer detailing who God is for me and to me.

In the gospel narratives, the Lord's Prayer is offered by Jesus before his experience of death and its consequences. As a prayer of Jesus's life in present time, it resonates with my own experience of life. But like all Christians, I receive the prayer after Jesus's death and its outcome. Thus, I read it as acknowledgement of what God has already done, is doing, and has committed to do in my life. It's a statement of how I believe God relates to me, of how I am related to God, from which perspective I encounter and relate to God.

The Kingdom

In the very first words of his prayer, Jesus encourages us to approach God as an innocent child. Children were of little status in many ancient cultures. A dependent child was not an asset until reaching an age to contribute to the common good. Children were beneath notice, much less comment. Even the infant Jesus makes only a brief appearance in a stable and is promptly whisked out of sight and danger, only to appear again among teachers in the temple at an age consistent with recognized maturity. To find a child in a gospel at all is remarkable. That a child should be for Jesus an icon of perfect humanity is so notably scandalous that the same story is recounted three times: in Matthew, Mark, and Luke.

Matthew tells how Jesus drew a child into a very adult argument about kingdoms, power, and glory to illustrate a central teaching: "He called a child, whom he put among them, and said, 'Truly I tell you, unless you change and become like children, you will never enter the kingdom of heaven. Whoever becomes humble like this child is the greatest in the kingdom of heaven. Whoever welcomes one such child in my name welcomes me'" (Matthew 18:2-5).

The Lord's Prayer begins with a naively intimate greeting of God as Abba. "Our Father" suggests the vast expanse of heaven—and a hallowing of the holy name—while simultaneously embracing an inseparable bond of affection and respect. God is as close as our literal next of kin, yet wholly separate and entirely God.

God's first attribute is kingship and God's asset is the kingdom, an archaic reference to earthly governance. Kingdom repeated in the concluding doxology fits the symmetry of kingdom in the opening declaration, "Your kingdom come." Quite apart from the gendered reference to male royal office in a role easily and often filled by a woman, kingship and kingdom are insufficient. We need larger words to express the fullness of God's sovereignty and authority.

Authority is rooted in the word author originator. To call God father, mother, or parent is to acknowledge God as the originator of one's life. Yet this claim upon God is shared with all who say this prayer. To claim God as Our Father historically anticipates and is consistent with the first principle of every Christian creed acknowledging God as Maker, Creator, Author of all things, seen and unseen.

Sovereignty in this instance proclaims God's realm as boundless, embracing all and everything.

God's realm is not bounded space: rather it is infinite and transparent. It's not a state of measured acres, numbered heads, herds, or human bodies and wills under control. It's a realm that one eucharistic prayer in the Book of Common Prayer describes as "the vast expanse of interstellar space, galaxies, suns, the planets in their courses, and this fragile earth, our island home," and everything beyond our knowing. We welcome and embrace that realm in the words, "Your kingdom come." We acknowledge the presence and reality of that realm in the ultimate proclamation, "the kingdom … is yours."

Jesus makes similar affirmations, assuring us that the kingdom is near at hand, that we're never far from it. Not distant and inaccessible but present, it is the very realm in which we "live and move and have our being" (Acts 17:28). We're always in the kingdom, the realm of God. We affirm its reality that we might recognize, know, and participate in that realm, that we may see it as God sees it—to see it, not to possess it, but to participate in it.

The Power

Power at its most basic is ability. The opening address to God in the Lord's Prayer is immediately followed by an affirmation of God's will as primary and universal: "your will be done, on earth as in heaven." This declaration is echoed in the closing doxology affirming God's ability as "the power." The potency and expanse of God's will is sufficient to accomplish God's purposes, utterly eclipsing human will.

Yet acknowledgment of God's potent will is not an endorsement of divine tyranny. This would be inconsistent with Jesus's encouraging us to approach God as worthy of the affectionate name Abba. Affection does not nullify obedience but is instead a genuine respect strengthened by willing cooperation. That Jesus was obedient to the will of God is not to say that Jesus was coerced into compliance by divine demand but rather that Jesus was motivated by trust to cooperate and work with God—to live a life consistent with God's will for every human being.

The word obey combines a prefix meaning toward and a verb meaning to hear. To obey is to lean into hearing, to listen intently so that speaker and hearer might find mutuality and union. Jesus's own habit of prayer is revealed most clearly in a moment of personal stress, the kind of situation in which one is less inclined to extemporaneous creativity than to established routine. As he kneels in Gethsemane, his life on the line, Jesus affirms, "Not my will but yours be done" (Luke 22:42; cf. Matthew 26:39, 42; Mark 14:36). Obedience, then, is an active listening such as Jesus exhibits. It's the active listening at the center of any collaboration between partners seeking a common outcome.

I was fortunate to have loving parents. But they were also stern parents. I was their firstborn, and we three were new to the business of being a family. They were older and larger than me and could do everything that I couldn't do. Late night screaming tantrums in a dark crib not only taught me that I could not coerce them into doing my will, but also taught them that we'd each survive the darkness enveloping all of us. Over many years we learned the delicate balance of freedom and responsibility as we worked at being human.

The Glory

Glory is too often confused with the blinding aura of celebrity within which modern imagination frames it. Glory is acknowledgment or praise, commendation, recognition, or just plain credit.

To paraphrase the first affirmation of our Christian creeds, God gets the credit for all that is, seen and unseen. To accord proper credit to any partner is an expression of mutual respect. Acknowledgement of and gratitude for God's gift of life in creation—to be grateful for our very existence—is consistent with a belief that God is indeed maker of all things. As such, God deserves the respect befitting a maker's primacy in relationship to what is made. Plainly, God was first. I came after. Jesus is said to have acknowledged as much; he "did not regard equality with

God as something to be exploited, but emptied himself" (Philippians 2:6-7). To accede to God's will and primacy is to practice the humility Jesus teaches in this prayer. Yet God's generosity tends toward mutuality, even in glory. As the first-century Greek bishop, Irenaeus, wrote, "the glory of God is the living human, and the life of human person is the vision of God."

A Trinity of Trinities

Give us today our daily bread…Forgive us our sins as we forgive those who sin against us…Save us from the time of trial and deliver us from evil. The Lord's Prayer is a study in trinities. An opening invocation and a concluding ascription bracket a set of three petitions of God, simultaneously affirming the gifts of God who provides for our physical sustenance, who forgives more generously than we do, and who grants us freedom to err and the grace to survive our errors.

Moreover, these three petitions subtly align with the three temptations set before Jesus in Mark's account (Mark 1:12-13) and more amply in the gospels of Luke (Luke 4:1-13) and Matthew (Matthew 4:1-11). Jesus is tempted to feed himself by turning stones to bread, to test the limits of God's care by throwing himself deliberately from the pinnacle of the temple, and to glorify himself by succumbing to the allure of earthly dominion. Intentionally or ironically, each temptation is echoed in a petition of the prayer he taught to his disciples. The temptations are echoed, too, in the introductory and concluding attributes imputed to God: authority (kingdom), ability (power), and accountability (glory).

After forty days of fasting, Jesus is tempted by Satan to turn stones into bread. In Matthew, Jesus asks, "Is there anyone among you who, if your child asks for bread, will give a stone? ... If you then, who are evil, know how to give good gifts to your children, how much more will your Father in heaven give good things to those who ask him!" (Matthew 7:9-11). Basic sustenance is a responsibility of parents and a reasonable expectation on the part of a dependent. This sustenance exemplifies the relationship of the Creator to all creatures. Moreover, in a creation amply providing for all creatures—a creation appointed with interdependent elements—expecting a stone to be transformed into bread isn't a miracle but rather an act of magic contravening nature's order.

That water was changed to wine at the wedding in Cana, as described in John (2:1-11), is not a contradiction of nature. Water taken into vines from the earth, squeezed from fruit, and allowed to age eventually becomes wine. The miracle in the story isn't in what happens to the water but what transpires in time. On the other hand, stones don't become bread under any circumstance. The Creator accepts authority and responsibility for the well-being of every creature.

When I utter the words, "Give us this day our daily bread," I affirm God's abundance. I am conscious that I've never truly been hungry, that I've always had more than enough bread to sustain me. I'm aware that God has truly fulfilled this need in my life; even to repeat these words is, for me, selfishness. Yet empathy compels me to acknowledge that I'm surrounded by siblings who are starving. Intellect and reason compel me to recognize that God has provided abundantly for us all—that hunger and starvation are not of God's will, but of mine. That I have the means to share and am thus obliged to do so is implicit.

---

*And forgive us … as we forgive….*The second temptation Jesus faced was the urge to test the limits of God's grace and care, to throw himself off the temple's height with full confidence that God would prevent his death. In truth, such a suicidal leap would not have proven God's potency so much as it would have validated human mental, physical, and spiritual frailty.

The irony of this test is that it was ultimately completed not in a selfish act of suicide but in a generous act of sacrifice. The tempter's test played upon Jesus's fear for his own life. It was a test hedged with limitations. It was a test limited to the protection of only one person, Jesus. It was a test limiting God's power only to prevent Jesus's death at that time, only forestalling the inevitable death that comes to every human being, even Jesus. It was too small a test, unworthy of undertaking. The death that comes to each of us came to Jesus in crucifixion, a death imposed by human force, embraced by human trust, endured by human love in Jesus.

The outcome was not a prevention of death but the potent endurance of life—not for one life alone, but for all.

When I request forgiveness extending only so far as I am prepared to give, I know this is too little. I know the truth of my own willful obstinacy, my intentional hurtfulness, and my accidental failures. That I live at all is testament to God's capacity being more than sufficient to embrace the whole of creation, to extend grace beyond our farthest imaginings, far exceeding my own ability to ask or know I ought to ask. I acknowledge that my own powers of forgiveness are limited, that God's forgiveness is more than my humanity allows. But neither can I rest upon my limitations as an excuse.

The third and final temptation Jesus confronted was to trust the tempter's offer of a vast realm to which only God holds the deed—and all for the low, low price of a tiny bit of respect. The tempter was taking credit far beyond his due by asking Jesus to trust a claim upon which the tempter could never deliver. You can't offer for sale what is not yours. Moreover, the tempter revealed a profound poverty in the price asked: genuine respect is earned, never bartered. This insidious trial is our daily lot. We live within systems dependent for their own perpetuity upon our insecurities. Modern politics, religion, capitalism, and more pique our fears and ply us with promises far beyond their capacity to keep. My personal insecurity is rooted in profound distrust of my own worth, my lovability. My thirst for validation is insatiable. I'm so prone to impulse, to the lures of empty promises and false claims, that I rarely recognize the extortion they commit. Is it because I have inherited and incorporated a deep distrust of humanity and my own embodiment that I find it so difficult to accept my inherent worth as a beloved creature of God?

All three of the temptations and their corresponding petitions in the Lord's Prayer touch upon human insecurity, the innate mistrust that undermines faith and poisons relationships. Distrust of God urges me to rely upon myself, pushes me to fill my plate beyond my appetite, fill my pantry beyond my need. Distrust of God enflames my fear of death, ruins my restful enjoyment of all God gives me, and pushes me to rush blindly past the bounty of friendship and love. Distrust of God erodes my self-confidence and confuses temporal success with genuine self-respect grounded in God's love—if and when I awake to it.

The Why: "For"

For the kingdom, the power, and the glory are yours, now and forever. Amen. The prologue of the Lord's Prayer addressing Abba, Our Father identifies the nature and being to whom we affirm relationship in our prayer. The three core petitions for sustenance, salvation, and security are expressed as we give and receive in our relationship with God. But the essential word in this epilogue to the Lord's Prayer is the three-letter conjunction for. Upon it hangs The Why. The word For in this context means because.

We address God as Abba, Father, Mother, Parent, and entrust our lives to God. As the Author of all things seen and unseen, God embodies absolute authority (the kingdom) because the record of our spiritual ancestors' testimony and our personal experience of life in all its abundance confirms God's consummate ability (the power). To God alone we grant credit and render gratitude for all we are, all we know, all we have now and all we shall be, know, and have forever, God possesses ultimate accountability (the glory).

Without God, we don't have a prayer. So we believe. So we are to live. *For the kingdom, the power, and the glory are yours, now and for ever. Amen.*

About the Editor

Rachel Jones loves Jesus, her husband, breakfast foods, and most cats. From 2014 to 2020, Rachel worked at Forward Movement. This book is a love letter to Jesus and in thanksgiving for all of it.

About the Authors

Cohen Adkins is a member of the Chickahominy Tribe in Virginia. Cohen is a graduate student in Indian law at the University of Tulsa and serves as the secretary for Region XIV of the Diocese of Virginia of the Episcopal Church. She has been a member of the Indigenous Women's Circle of Indigenous Ministries and worked as a research and communication consultant for the Office of Indigenous Ministries. She currently serves on the Native American Ministry Commission of the Diocese of Virginia and attended the United Nations Permanent Forum on Indigenous Issues 2015 as a delegate of the Episcopal Church.

Ryan Black is the head of Legal Operations for Opendoor. Ryan has focused his career on helping legal departments run smarter during periods of hyper-growth and on implementing right-sized technology solutions that automate routine processes and provide meaningful data about how teams are working. Outside of the office, Ryan enjoys running, reading, cooking, and playing with his cats. He worships with the good people at Saint Gregory of Nyssa in San Francisco, California.

James Derkits lives, loves, and ministers in the Texas Gulf Coast. He and his wife, Laura Jane are the proud parents of Eli. They worship and work alongside the people of Trinity by the Sea in Port Aransas, Texas. James loves playing guitar, surfing, and making things. You can hear more of his work by checking out his two most recent albums, *Love One Another* (2020) and *Buffalo Roam* (2016). He has also written for *Forward Day by Day*.

Elizabeth DeRuff is an agricultural chaplain with the Episcopal Church, businesswoman, and farmer who makes her home in Marin County, California. She is a pioneer in exploring the intersection of food, land, and faith. In this capacity, she conducts research, writes, teaches, preaches, and consults with congregations around the country. Currently, Elizabeth grows and sources two varieties of heirloom wheat, which are stone-milled and available for sale from Honoré Farm and Mill.

Miriam McKenney is a beloved child of God residing in Cincinnati, Ohio. Wife to David and mother to Nia, Kaia, and Jayia, Miriam relishes time with her family and loves being outdoors. The director of development and community engagement at Forward Movement, she is an active member of the Union of Black Episcopalians, Episcopal Communicators, the Way of Love, Becoming Beloved Community, and the Commission on Ministry for the Diocese of Southern Ohio. She also enjoys the company of her cats, Spencer and Winston. You can read more from Miriam in *Are We There Yet?* and *Waiting and Watching: Advent Word Reflections*, both by Forward Movement. She has also written for *Forward Day by Day*.

Catherine Meeks is the executive director of the Absalom Jones Center for Racial Healing. Prior to the center's opening she chaired its precursor, Beloved Community: Commission for Dismantling Racism for the Episcopal Diocese of Atlanta. A teacher and workshop leader, Catherine brings four decades of experience to the work of transforming the dismantling racism work in Atlanta. The core of her work has been with people who have been marginalized because of economic status, race, gender, or physical ability as they pursue liberation, justice, and access to resources that can help lead them to health, wellness, and a more abundant life. This work grows out of her understanding of her call to the vocation of teacher as well as her realization that all of humanity is one family which God desires to unite.

Sandra Montes is an active preacher, teacher, and vocalist across the Episcopal Church. Currently serving as dean of chapel at Union Theological Seminary, Sandra is passionate about leading worship that is honest, thoughtful, joyful, and liberating. You can read more from Sandra in *Abiding with God: Day by Day* from Forward Movement. She has also written for *Forward Day by Day.* Her latest title, *Becoming Real*, is available from Church Publishing.

Sam Portaro is a retired priest of the Episcopal Church. He served as vicar of the Church of the Epiphany in Newton, North Carolina, Episcopal chaplain to the College of William & Mary, and associate rector of Bruton Parish Church in Williamsburg, Virginia, from 1976 until 1982, and Episcopal chaplain and director of Brent House at The University of Chicago, 1982-2004. From 2005 to 2017, he served on conference faculty and wrote for CREDO, the education and wellness division of the Church Pension Group. Author of eight books and numerous essays and articles, he conducts quiet days and retreats, and has served as a consultant, educator, and preacher. He lives in Chicago with his spouse, Christopher Dionesotes, with whom he enjoys cooking, music, theater, movies, reading, and the city's endless cultural and culinary bounty.

About Forward Movement

Forward Movement is committed to inspiring disciples and empowering evangelists. While we produce great resources like this book, Forward Movement is more than a publishing company. We are a ministry.

We live out this ministry through publishing books, daily reflections, studies for small groups, and online resources. More than a half million people read our daily devotions through *Forward Day by Day,* which is also available in Spanish (*Adelante Día a Día*) and Braille, online, as a podcast, and as an app for your smartphones or tablets. It is mailed to more than fifty countries, and we donate nearly 30,000 copies each quarter to prisons, hospitals, and nursing homes. We actively seek partners across the church and look for ways to provide resources that inspire and challenge. A ministry of the Episcopal Church for more than eighty years, Forward Movement is a nonprofit organization funded by sales of resources and gifts from generous donors.

To learn more about Forward Movement and our resources, visit forwardmovement.org or venadelante.org. We are delighted to be doing this work and invite your prayers and support.